THE PROSPERITY GAME

THE PROSPERITY GAME

Four Steps to Unlimited Wealth

Richard A. Fishman and
Charles P. Werner, Esq.

NEW YORK

THE PROSPERITY GAME
Four Steps to Unlimited Wealth

ISBN 978-1-61448-580-3 paperback
ISBN 978-1-61448-581-0 eBook
ISBN 978-1-61448-582-7 audio
Library of Congress Control Number: 2013932145

Morgan James Publishing
The Entrepreneurial Publisher
5 Penn Plaza, 23rd Floor
New York City, New York 10001
(212) 655-5470 office • (516) 908-4496 fax
www.MorganJamesPublishing.com

Cover Design by:
Rachel Lopez
www.r2cdesign.com

Interior Design by:
Bonnie Bushman
bonnie@caboodlegraphics.com

TABLE OF CONTENTS

FOREWORD

Historically, any favorable characterization of the American economic system has always included the strong spirit of entrepreneurship. There is something attractive and seductive when an individual can build from the very beginning and watch that creation survive, grow and even become the best in a highly competitive marketplace. Admittedly, many men and women are satisfied to be average and non-achievers and there certainly is a suitable place in business for this level of ambition and competency. Fortunately, however, many others strive to be super-achievers…to mold an idea into a cause, company, product or service that carries an extraordinary human imprint and inventory, is successful and truly matters in the scheme of things.

Inasmuch as we only have one life to live, I believe it is critical that we seize every opportunity to maximize our focus and priorities, our skills and talent, our personal and professional worth, our sense of what worthwhile deeds we can accomplish in the space that we occupy. It is important to be sensitive to how mankind remembers us. A successful job or a profitable business allows us to help others in a meaningful way and sometimes with minimum sacrifice. It is a healthy thing that in our country every needed company has not already been formed, every service fine-tuned, every human appetite gratified, every gadget invented, every medical answer uncovered. In short, we desperately seek the entrepreneur whose dimensions can be shaped and nurtured and who is willing to take the risk and climb the highest mountain. Why be content to be like most others?

Fundamental to the achiever is identifying where there remains a vacuum to be filled and what ability, knowledge and experience he or she possesses to make a difference. Yes, a sound business plan must be crafted - one that is realistic and relevant, one that respects expert management and marketing, one that takes full advantage of education and the practical. Perhaps most important, however, there must also be commitment, energy and passion. We have a better chance of meeting challenges and overcoming serious obstacles if there is a fervent personal desire to succeed. No one can deprive you of an attitude that demands to be productive and profitable.

Realize it or not, every company, firm or nonprofit has a personality. And that culture clearly reflects the persona of the chief executive or entrepreneur at the top. An entity that is built on integrity, practices the finest quality of ethics and is mindful of inflexible standards has taken the first step toward success. Business is littered with shortcuts and temptation; so is life itself. If who we are and what we do is beyond legitimate criticism and scorn, it is easier to reach out to customers and clients, investors and staff, media and the government. No one suggests that this journey is free of heartache and pain – but the ease of living comfortably with yourself and with others is a prize worth pursuing. And the community and corporate goodwill generated by honest behavior is a valuable commodity.

How you treat your staff, for example, is vivid evidence of the recognition you assign teamwork in reaching your financial goals. It doesn't take much to be decent, to show personnel admiration, affection and appreciation. Several years ago the Thanksgiving, Christmas and New Year's holidays all fell on Thursdays, in each case leaving an awkward and obscure Friday before the weekend. I strongly recommended that my client give his employees each of the three Fridays off as a gift. Frankly, I figured little work could be accomplished after a holiday. Initially, he resisted; he then pondered and ultimately closed shop for the Fridays. He couldn't contact me fast enough to brag with tremendous pride about this generosity and perceived thoughtfulness toward his staff. And then he naively added: "Of course, I deducted each Friday from their paychecks." Really!

How a client treats his consultant is also the tenor of a positive relationship. Each year my public relations firm gives staff the days off between Christmas and New Years as a holiday gift. We only require associates to notify clients of this arrangement leaving appropriate telephone numbers in case of an emergency. One of my clients was sufficiently impressed with our gesture to call me to exclaim: "What a fantastic tradition. However, inasmuch as you and your staff will not be servicing me during the holidays, I am sending you my usual December retainer <u>minus</u> one week. If they're on vacation, they surely can't be helping me." Really!

In contrast that same week another client sent us a totally unexpected bonus "just to say thanks for all you have done for my company this year." Which of the two really motivated us for the future?

As I reflect on the hazardous business climate of the day, I am not ashamed of the country of my birth, the Armenian heritage of my parents and the Christian faith of my household. On the contrary, I am extremely grateful for, and proud of, an exciting and rewarding way of life that allowed me to begin a practice in 1969 with two clients that now exceeds a legacy of more than 5,000. What a privilege to serve others within the framework of a profitable business. What joy to partake of all this with God as my partner. He doesn't guarantee success but stands by my side as I strive to achieve it. We are taught that smart management and marketing, that strict adherence to careful planning and well-defined objectives, that respect for substantial resources and a little bit of luck, that the wise counsel and loyalty of friends and experts...can help ensure success. Let this strength be influenced by the caring, wisdom and power of God and faith, and watch your balance sheet leap beyond your wildest expectation. Read carefully the profound interviews in this book with thirteen achievers who reject mediocrity and instead magnificently blend business and faith to attain heights of true accomplishment, and then invite the pages of *The Prosperity Game* to impact your present and your tomorrow.

Carl R. Terzian
Los Angeles, California
September 10, 2012

INTRODUCTION

Is there a universal path to success?

For many people, success can be elusive—both conceptually and as a personal experience. Depending on who you listen to, success is achieved in different ways.

Rhonda Byrne, author of *The Secret,*[1] asserts that it is all about the law of attraction—whatever you think about you will attract into your life. By understanding and utilizing the power of thought, people can create whatever they want in their lives, be it better relationships, greater prosperity, or vibrant health.

Malcolm Gladwell, author of *Outliers: The Story of Success,*[2] approaches the matter analytically. He studied the lives of extremely successful people to determine what it was that led to their success. Based upon these investigations, Gladwell asserts that successful people are those who are both given the opportunities and willing to work the hardest.

For some, the path to success is an inside job. For others, it is the result of what happens in the external world. It is our belief that mastery of both inner and outer circumstances will propel you down the road to success.

We have achieved worldly success and are passionate about sharing our knowledge to help you create a life filled with material abundance. During the course of writing this book, we interviewed other successful business people—all millionaires, some many times over. Their stories provide inspiration, convey useful information, and vividly demonstrate that there is a specific set of principles that reliably lead to success.

Four Steps to Success

Based upon our own personal experience—and that of our highly successful interviewees—we have developed a simple, four-step approach to success that anyone can utilize. By applying these four simple, yet powerful principles, you can manifest material abundance. These principles have always existed - just waiting to be discovered and shared with you.

Our four-step process includes the laws of thought, inspiration, planning, and commitment. As with the other laws that govern life on Earth, such as Newton's law of universal gravitation and Einstein's theory of general relativity, these laws are scientific and immutable.

Chapter 1 provides a brief overview of the four steps and the subsequent chapters explain in detail how to implement each step.

The Prosperity Game

While everyone who follows these four steps will meet with some level of success, you can supercharge your efforts by consciously understanding and working with the power that resides at the core of *The Prosperity Game*. When you tap into the source of all that is, your higher power, the God of your understanding, you become unstoppable. Be open to guidance from within and without, as you implement each of the four steps for developing your business.

The spiritual and material realms share a common foundation—a single set of laws underlies both. When you make your business a *divine* business, you open yourself and your business to previously undreamed of possibilities and rewards far beyond anything that can be obtained through personal effort alone. God—your ultimate source, your higher power—is the best possible business partner. *The Prosperity Game* will take you on a spiritual journey that combines meaningful personal growth with practical knowledge about how you can achieve prosperity in the material world.

We hope you enjoy—and profit—from your quest.

THE SPIRITUAL AND THE MATERIAL—ONE WORLD OR TWO?

CHAPTER 1

D o you dream of attaining inner and outer riches? Can you have a great spiritual life while enjoying fabulous wealth? Is such a life possible?

If you think a life filled with spiritual and material wealth is merely a fantasy, you are not alone. Some people believe they must choose either an outer life of material abundance gained by participation in the world, or an inner life of spiritual abundance gained by deepening their relationship with God.

Is this belief in such a material/spiritual choice built upon a solid foundation or simply an outdated concept? History is replete with examples of beliefs once universally accepted as true but now known to be false. Today we know that the earth is not the center of the universe. Nor is it flat.

The spiritual millionaires you will soon meet are living proof that your house need not be divided. Both God and material abundance may be realized here and now, in this world. Indeed, if you are to fulfill your potential as a human being, you must be fully engaged in every possible facet of existence—the divine and worldly, the intangible and tangible, the spiritual and material.

You might be thinking "Wait a minute, I'm not buying this." Many people remain firmly convinced that economic Darwinism determines who becomes rich—that in this materialistic jungle, only the most aggressive prosper. Hard-core capitalists—whose sole interest is making money without regard for moral or spiritual considerations—sit at the pinnacle of financial abundance. Anyone who attempts to apply spiritual ideals in their material life will be trampled underfoot by these unbridled capitalists.

There is substantial evidence that these widely held beliefs are mistaken. Alex Edmans, an Assistant Professor of Finance at the Wharton School, University of Pennsylvania, authored a study in August, 2012, which documented that treating your employees well results in increased stock prices for your company. Mr. Edmans concluded that "firms with high levels of job satisfaction, as measured by inclusion in the list of the "Best Companies to Work For in America", generate high long-run stock returns." Specifically, the "Companies listed in the "100 Best Companies to Work For in America" generated 2.3-3.8%/year higher stock returns than their peers from 1984-2011." Alex Edmans also found that "the Best Companies systematically beat analyst earnings estimates".[3] Doing good pays dividends.

In early summer 2011 Towers Watson conducted its 2011/2012 North American Talent Management and Reward Survey and the results parallel the findings of Alex Edmans. "Organizations with reward and talent management programs that support their business goals are more than twice as likely to report being high-performing companies (28% versus 12%).

Those with reward and talent management programs that support their attraction and retention goals are less likely to report having trouble attracting critical skill employees (52% versus 68%) or retaining critical skill employees (29% versus 43%)."[4] Treating employees well through reward and talent management programs will make it easier for you to recruit and retain critical skill employees and well-treated employees are motivated to make your business a high-performing company.

When Chris Van Gorder became the CEO of Scripps Health in 2000, it was a large hospital system characterized by operating losses in excess of $20 million per year, high turnover and labor shortages, union and legislative risk. Chris Van Gorder and Senior Vice President Vic Buzachero created a turnaround program that focused on Scripps' workforce. The Scripps' management team utilized the services of Great Place to Work® as a major component of the turnaround program.

Great Place to Work® took a multifaceted approach, which included a system-wide survey of all employees using Great Place to Work® methodology, analysis of the survey results and recommendations for improvement. Each year thereafter Great Place to Work® analyzed Scripps' performance and recommended specific areas to be improved.

Through analyzing data, Scripps discovered a relationship between the Scripps performance management system scores of individual managers and the Great Place to Work® survey results of the employees who worked for those managers. Scripps divided management performance into quarters and found that managers in the top quarter of Great Place to Work® results performed significantly better than those in the bottom quarter. On average, the departments lead by the top quarter managers had 0% budget variance while the bottom quarter managers had a negative 8.7%

budget variance. The departments lead by top quarter managers had a 5.6% turnover rate while the bottom quarter managers had a 16.6% turnover rate.

How has this kinder, gentler approach been working out for Scripps? Scripps has seen dramatic improvements in financial performance, turnover rates and employee morale. Over the past 10 years, employee survey results have improved by 54% while the system has realized over $70 million in cost savings and increased its annual profits by over 1200%. Scripps accomplished this turnaround by making a commitment to transform their workplace culture in addition to focusing on their system's financial performance.[5] If you want your employees to be more productive, give them the working environment you would like. Being a good employer is smart business.

Dramatic examples of good guys finishing first were played out before worldwide audiences in Super Bowls XLII and XLVI. Twice the New England Patriots and New York Giants met in football's biggest game and twice the Giants prevailed.

Super Bowl XLII was played on Sunday, February 3, 2008. The seemingly invincible New England Patriots arrived at the game with an 18-0 record. Their opponents, the New York Giants, had lost six games in the regular season and were trying to become only the second wild-card team ever to win the Super Bowl. The Patriots were heavy favorites—not simply to win, but to *crush* the Giants.

It didn't happen quite that way. With less than two minutes left in the game and down 14-10, the Giants got the ball back. Michael Strahan, the emotional sparkplug of the Giants, strode up and down the New York bench. "17-14!" he shouted. "We can do this!" And they did! In less than two minutes, the Giants drove the ball 83 yards and scored a touchdown. By believing in themselves, the unsung Giants were able to beat the Patriots for the biggest upset in Super Bowl history.

So what does a football game have to do with good guys finishing first? Quite a lot, as it turns out. In the first game of the 2007 regular season, the Patriots were caught stealing the signals of the opposing team with a video camera. During the investigation that followed, Bill Belichick admitted he had been filming the opposing team's offensive and defensive signals regularly since becoming New England's head coach in 2000. While the Patriot coaches and management tried to make light of the filming, the league was not so inclined. The NFL slapped a $500,000 fine on Belichick, another $250,000 fine on the Patriots, and it took away the team's first-round pick in the 2008 NFL draft.

The behavior of the Patriots is in stark contrast to the humility displayed by the Giants personnel in their post-game interviews. Head coach Tom Coughlin complimented the New England Patriots, calling them a great team. Quarterback Eli Manning talked about the catches made by his receivers during the game-winning drive. Michael Strahan, the cornerstone of the Giants defense, said "My guys are the best in the world." And it turns out they were—shutting down the number-one offense in the history of the NFL. In interview after interview, when the Giants players were asked about their personal accomplishments in the game, they talked about their teammates, not themselves.

Fast forward to Super Bowl XLVI played on Sunday, February 8, 2012. The New England Patriots entered the game with a 15-3 record. Again the New York Giants were a wild card team, having lost seven games in the regular season. Just a few weeks earlier, after a week 15 loss to the Washington Redskins, the Giants sat at 7-7, and were on the brink of missing the postseason. The Giants then reeled off five straight wins, including beating two of the best teams in the NFL in the playoffs - the Green Bay Packers and San Francisco 49ers - to enter the Super Bowl with a 12 –7 record.

The Giants' capped off their improbable run with one last comeback to defeat the New England Patriots 21-17 in Super Bowl XLVI. Down 17-15 with 3 minutes and 46 seconds left in the game, New York took over at its own 12 yard line. The team drove the ball down the field in less than 3 minutes and scored the game-winning touchdown.

After the game a reporter commented to New York quarterback Eli Manning that only 11 quarterbacks had won two Super Bowls and he was now one of them. Manning replied, "I don't think that's the story. The story is the New York Giants won the championship. This isn't about one person. This is about a team coming together."

Justin Tuck, a defensive stalwart for the Giants who had two sacks in the game echoed those sentiments, saying "This was a team effort, a team win."

Tom Coughlin, the embattled coach of the New York Giants who was on the hot seat all season long, summed it up with these words, "All things are possible for those who believe." Coughlin was either consciously or unconsciously paraphrasing the words of Jesus.

There are immutable divine laws at work here, regardless of whether we believe in them or are even aware of their existence. These divine laws include techniques for achieving success in the world.

So, what are these techniques? They are a simple adaptation of the four-step process God used to create the universe. You can achieve success by utilizing this four-step approach, which we will summarize in the remainder of this chapter. Subsequent chapters are devoted to a detailed explanation of the four steps, and will provide you with exercises and tools to help you effectively implement each step. Through the practical application of these principles, you will personally reap the richest harvest of spiritual *and* material success.

Your dreams can and will become reality.

Step One: Find and Develop Your Seed Thought

What is a seed thought? How will my seed thought come to me?

Our story begins at the beginning. We mean at the *very* beginning—what the Bible calls *Genesis*. The origin of the universe is called the *Big Bang* by scientists, but even before that split second of incomparable energy, there was the foundational thought of God. Everything around us has its origin in that unknowable Great Mind.

Energy spewed forth in response to that Divine thought. The Divine will then molded that energy to form our world. From its very inception, our cosmos has been guided by this Divine universal pattern. It begins with thought, moves into energy, and results in a physical manifestation created through willpower. This Divine formula is the template for all creation, including the creation of wealth.

Man being made in God's image is not just a metaphor, but the very foundation of who we are. Man, alone in our world, was given the Divine power to manifest his thoughts and aspirations as physical reality. Like Michael Strahan, we all use our thoughts as the springboard to make things happen here on Earth. The proof can be found in the manmade world all around us.

The first step in all creative endeavors is to come up with an idea, because all action begins with thought. Some thoughts are more inspired than others. Those thoughts which come from your intuition—your highest source of consciousness—may rightly be called *seed thoughts*.

A seed thought = the manifestation of Spirit as an idea

We use the equal sign to indicate that we are speaking of a science every bit as powerful and practical as physics or chemistry. Your seed thought contains the building blocks—the DNA—of what you desire to create.

A seed thought expands beyond the actual words and merges with the intention behind the words—the feelings around the words and the entire being of the person having the thought. Seed thoughts have a dynamic power well beyond your normal everyday thoughts. They are born in your consciousness to help you fulfill your divinely ordained mission on Earth.

There is a unique seed thought for you, for me, for every one of us. Our interviewees discovered and developed their seed thoughts in a variety of ways. Edna Hennessee's seed thought arose from a practical desire to overcome her personal challenges. Zachary Taylor consciously developed a seed thought incubation process that harnesses the tremendous power of the subconscious mind. Both of these approaches and others will be discussed in detail in chapter 2, where we provide you with tools to help you find your seed thought.

Possession of a seed thought, though empowering in and of itself, does not guarantee success in the world. Before you attempt to implement your idea, you must analyze it. Does it look and feel right to you? Does it ring true? Does it fit with your world view? Is the thought practical and do you have the skills needed to turn this idea into a business? If all of these questions are answered in the affirmative, you move on to the second step, determining whether this seed thought is your calling from God.

Step Two: Determine and Accept Your Calling

What is a calling? How do I find my calling?

Some people have a restrictive definition of what it means to be called by the Divine, but Spirit is infinitely creative. Our roles come in all shapes and sizes. This diversity is reflected by the fact that everyone has a special calling.

While your calling may not be to spread the gospel or feed the lepers of Calcutta, it is no less important. The people interviewed for *The Prosperity Game* have been called to follow many different paths: create a public relations firm, manufacture clothing, develop and produce documentary films, provide medical equipment, manufacture herbal teas and design forecasting software for businesses.

So what exactly is a *calling*? Your calling is simply the place where you feel totally alive and connected to all that is. Through being receptive to inspiration and guidance, whether from within or without, your mission will come into focus. When you open a channel to the spiritual realms, your activities and aspirations are infused with divine energy. Personal goals and desires are shaped to serve the grand design and life becomes filled with meaning.

How can you become more receptive to this divine plan? No one method of making a connection with the divine is better than any other method. Some methods, such as meditation, being in nature, or prayer, work well for many people but not for everyone. No matter what your makeup, there is a way to attune with Spirit that will work well for you. In chapter 3, we provide simple processes to deepen your unique relationship with the Divine.

For a few fortunate individuals, such as Drake Sadler, their calling makes itself known in a dramatic fashion. For many others, including Kim Gay, their calling comes into focus over a period of time. Your calling may announce itself in either of these ways, or in a thousand others.

So, how do you know that your seed thought is your calling? In the end, it is a matter of heart. Pay attention to how you feel after immersing yourself in your seed thought. If your seed thought reflects your true calling, you will feel connected, passionately alive and totally present in the moment.

Many believe that spiritual people have given up all passion. This could not be further from the truth. Passion and spirituality are intimate partners. Jesus was very passionate about his message. St. Francis, Mother Teresa, Albert Schweitzer and many others who found their calling, were equally passionate about their mission in life. You need passion to access the power of Spirit in your business, to live your calling, to follow your bliss.

When you recognize your calling, you know there your life has a purpose, there is a reason why you are here. Your heaven-sent thought now infuses you with Divine energy and deep peace. You become more fully engaged with life. You are surrounded by an all-pervading sense of well-being and the inherent perfection of everything. When you embrace your seed thought, you open the door to tremendous external achievement and deep inner fulfillment. You have found your calling, what you were meant to do. Your life becomes what it was always meant to be—a gift from the Divine will.

When you accept your calling, the standoff between heaven and earth has ended. Your business is united with your spiritual life. You feel the grace of the Divine as you reach for your goals of material *and* spiritual abundance. You are on your way, but there is still a lot of work to do. Now it is time to manifest your calling in the world.

Step Three: Ground Your Calling in the World

How do you turn your calling into material abundance? Is it really necessary to plan for success?

Your seed thought has descended from the realm of Spirit and has become your calling, filling you with energy and enthusiasm. Yet, at this point, it is still just a seed. Every seed needs fertile soil to grow into a strong presence in the world. To implement this divine plan for your life, practical steps must be taken to turn your idea into a thriving business. We call this third step "grounding your calling in the world."

Once you have accepted your calling, you have a destination but no clear path to take you there. Few people would explore an unfamiliar city without a map, yet many people do exactly that when starting a business. They discover a wonderful idea that fills them with enthusiasm, but fail in business simply because they do not develop a map to help them reach their goal.

One of the key elements of that map is planning. Solid planning accompanies every successful enterprise. The old adage, "Those who fail to plan, plan to fail," is as true for a spiritually inspired and guided business as it is for any other kind of company. A myriad of practical details must be considered in the process of creating a business.

How do you create the practical foundation for your spiritual business?

The people we interviewed approached the process in a variety of ways. Ali Kiran created a formal business plan and tapped a group of CEOs for advice. Mark Myers set very specific, written, attainable goals and methodically completed the tasks necessary to reach those goals. Patty DeDominic learned the ropes by working for major corporations and subsequently was invited to become a partner in a company, where she gained hands-on experience in running a business.

The oft-repeated phrase, "environment is stronger than willpower," holds true in the business world. If you want your business to prosper, surround yourself with advisors who are successful people. The sources of advice used by our interviewees include seminars, consultants, trade associations, and boards of directors. Take classes wherever you can: be a student of your business and of life.

Our spiritual millionaires have used additional techniques to turn their seed thoughts into reality. Among those tools are carrying inspirational phrases or articles in their wallets and studying good and bad role models.

If you want true abundance, however, it is helpful to plan your personal life in addition to your business activities. This business and personal planning, which we call your *Homework*, helps integrate your spiritual goals and personal commitments with your business. Your Homework maps out how you will live your life—24 hours a day, 7 days a week.

You now have the tools you need to help turn your business vision into a successful enterprise. One last step remains. To assure your success, you need to tap into your deepest resources, both within and without. You need to be fully committed to your business.

Step Four: Make The Commitment

Do you really have to make a personal commitment? Does making a commitment to God add anything of value to your pursuit of wealth?

Commitment is a necessary ingredient in every successful business enterprise. Why? This familiar maxim says it best—

"when the going gets tough, the tough get going." We can assure you that the going will get tough on your road to prosperity. It always does. Every millionaire will tell you they reached a point in their business where they wondered why they were doing it and whether they should go on. Yet, they persevered and reaped the rewards of success.

Everyone who has ever been successful made a tangible commitment to themselves to attain their personal goals. Many people have attained great success by following the laws of thought, inspiration, planning, and commitment. You, too, must make a personal commitment to create a thriving company based on your seed thought. We hope you now understand the value of making this commitment to yourself. It provides the unshakable foundation upon which you will build your business.

So, personal commitment is a must in the business world. Why then should you make a similar commitment to the Divine? Both your inner and outer lives will be greatly enriched by joining them together. Your goals will be achieved more quickly and easily when your spiritual and material energies work in unison.

Chapter 5 includes a contract for you to declare your personal commitment to your business, and a covenant that affirms your spiritual commitment to your business. Within these agreements lies a hidden power far beyond the words they contain. This written commitment, the true "Secret," is often the difference between success and failure.

Each of us has a sacred, personal relationship with the Divine and we express that relationship individually. This uniqueness is beautifully expressed in the words of our interviewees, each of whom relates to and talks about divinity in a decidedly different, personal way. It is all about first discovering what is personally true for you and then living in that truth.

Open yourself to the vast possibilities of co-creation with the divine that are your unique contributions to life. Discover the divine laws of creation which underlie material *and* spiritual success, and utilize them to attain great wealth, both in the outer world of business and in the quiet, inner realm of the soul.

STEP ONE—FIND AND DEVELOP YOUR SEED THOUGHT

CHAPTER 2

And the earth was without form, and void ... And God said let there be light and there was light. (Genesis 1:2-3)

Every successful enterprise has four components: the seed thought, the calling, the grounding, and the commitments. These four elements directly correspond to the four realms into which God divided His creation: thought, energy, matter, and free will.

The four realms of God's creation	The four elements of a successful business
Thought	Seed Thought
Energy	Calling
Matter	Grounding
Free will	Commitments

Your first task is to understand and utilize the power of thought, which governs the success of all your ventures. Where does thought come from? The first chapter of the book of Genesis in the Bible gives us a clue. Where did God begin when the world was created? In a place without form. That is where you should also begin when you want to obtain a seed thought. Ironically, this seemingly empty space is the home of all possibilities. Every idea that has ever been or ever will be thought has its origin in this void, this great abyss, this state of being. It is here that all creativity begins.

> *The universe emerges out of the all-nourishing abyss not only twelve billion years ago but in every moment. The foundational reality of the universe is this unseen ocean of potentiality.*
> —Brian Swimme[6]

While you may not be interested in creating a new cosmos, you might want to fashion a prosperous and meaningful life. Your path to abundance begins with accessing God's central storehouse of ideas. How do you do this? By going within— into that quiet place where your soul resides. From this place of peace, contentment, and joy, you can receive your seed thought. With your seed thought in hand, the process of divinely inspired creation is on its way!

Let's look at the role of thought in creation from another, more prosaic perspective. Imagine starting a business without an initial mental impression of what you want to achieve. Does this exercise seem impossible? That's because it is. Successful action in this world begins with thought. Even if you are working for someone else on their idea, that particular idea is the foundation for your work. You have to "buy in" to the endeavor if you are going to be a productive member of the team.

Your seed thought contains the complete template for the growth of your business—the DNA for your success in the world. Just as DNA guides and uses various elements in the world to create a plant or a person, your seed thought both influences and enlists the aid of your intentions and emotions. Your seed thought utilizes many of your resources and continues to grow until it pervades your awareness.

Your seed thought is also shaped by who you are. This is an interactive process in which you and your creation are constantly communicating and evolving together. Great artists understand this intensely personal relationship. The marble slab that eventually became his *David* had been in Michelangelo's possession for years, but he refused to work with it. Michelangelo said the stone was already alive with its creation, and he needed to listen to it until the image became clear.

Your unique nature and seed thought will also communicate with each other and grow together. Through this process your seed thought will become deeply personal and a clear path will emerge.

We often hear an inventor or entrepreneur claim "This is *my* idea," or "Only *I* could have created this." Such an ego-based claim to originality is only partially true. These people would be more correct if they claimed, "I was the first to receive this idea and manifest it." Each inventor and entrepreneur simply tunes into the essence of a particular seed thought. A person receives the seed thought meant for him or her in the same way that a tuning fork responds to one specific note.

When you receive your seed thought, it is an as-yet-unmanifested possible future. However, your seed thought is not merely a blueprint—it also contains tremendous energy combined with an intelligent force. This force is non-judgmental, neutral, powerful, and indomitable and will assist you in manifesting your purpose. Since we are made in God's image, we are able to create our reality from thought, just as God created this world from His thought.

The power of thought and how it becomes reality is discussed in the sacred texts of all world religions. There are many passages in both the Old and New Testament of the Bible that refer to this divine dynamo of thought. "So shall my word be that goes forth out of my mouth: it shall not return unto me void, but it shall accomplish that which I please, and it shall prosper in the thing whereto I sent it." (Isaiah 55:11).

What is a Seed Thought?

So, what then is a seed thought? As you will recall from our introduction to the concept of a seed thought in chapter 1:

A seed thought = the manifestation of Spirit as an idea

The path to material and spiritual abundance begins with your seed thought and is a journey guided by the laws of science. Science, you say? So far, all of this stuff seems to be metaphysical or religious rhetoric, and theoretical, at best. Right?

Many people think that quantum physics is theoretical, yet quantum theory has had a tremendous impact on our day-to-day world. In the words of Bruce Rosenblum and Fred Kuttner, "Much of modern technology is based on devices designed with quantum mechanics… One-third of our economy depends on products based on it."[7]

So quantum physics is practical. What does this have to do with finding your seed thought?

According to quantum physics, the consciousness of the observer creates the physical reality they experience. Rosenblum and Kuttner state, "[I]n one experiment, an atom can be shown to be a compact, concentrated thing, but with a different experiment, you could have shown that atom to be spread out over a wide region."[8]

In other words, if you look for a particle, you find a particle, and if you look for a wave, you find a wave. What you think creates what you observe. Thought creates your world.

Is that scientific enough for you?

These laws are as mathematically binding as the law of gravity. If you drop a hammer on your toe, you do not argue with gravity. If you fail at a business enterprise, do not blame external factors. If you accept the laws of science or the teachings of any of the great spiritual traditions, there is no room for chance. As Albert Einstein said, "God does not play dice with the Universe."

Where Do Seed Thoughts Come From?

When we were children, the world was a very mysterious place. We often did not understand the cause-and-effect relationships around us. As adults, we understand that a seed grows into a plant, and that a baby kitten becomes a cat. Although we now have no trouble understanding the progression of life in plants or animals, we often have difficulty envisioning the results of our thoughts.

Why is this so?

One reason is that we are seldom aware of more than a few of the thousands of thoughts we experience while awake each day and are even less aware of the thoughts we have while asleep. Nevertheless, our thoughts do come to fruition over time and determine just about everything we feel, see, and do. These thoughts sculpt our inner environment which in turn, becomes the controlling factor in our outer lives.

There is an old saying often credited to Abraham Lincoln which goes something like this: "At twenty, we have the face that God gave us. At thirty, we have the face that life gave us. At forty, we have the face we gave ourselves." This quotation underscores that, over time, your choices create your life.

Yet, your thoughts are not solely the creation of your own mind. Some thoughts come from within you, while other thoughts are picked up from the people around you or arise from the collective unconscious. Ultimately, of course, all thoughts are divine. How could it be otherwise? God is all that is.

When Moses asked for God's Name, God replied "I am that I am." (Exodus 3:14). God exists in that place where all potential resides—in the void, the abyss, the state of being. Every thought—whether in the past, present, or future—is eternally alive in the Divine mind.

God's dominion over the realm of thought can be seen in the world of science. Competing scientists, unaware of one another's work, have often made the same discovery at nearly the same time. This was true long before scientists had access to the Internet or, for that matter, any electronic communication at all.

In fact, the history of science is filled with disputes over who first made a particular discovery. One such dispute arose between Isaac Newton and Gottfried Wilhelm Leibniz. Each independently developed the mathematics we now call *calculus*. How does this happen? These scientists, hundreds of miles apart, tuned into the Divine storehouse and received the same seed thought at virtually the same instant.

You, too, can reach into this spiritual storehouse. Jesus said "Ask, and it shall be given you; seek, and you shall find; knock, and it shall be opened to you." (Matthew 7:7). While you may not pray in the traditional sense, it is likely that you have thought long and hard about a problem that confronted you. Were you surprised when the answer came into your mind after you had put the problem aside and relaxed—when you gave it a rest?

The process is actually quite simple. First, you sought an answer to your question or problem by knocking on the door of the Divine storehouse, by tapping into the source of all that is. Then, when you relaxed, you became receptive to the answer and it was given to you.

Since this process happens quite frequently in our lives, we take it for granted and barely notice it. But should we be so oblivious? You reached into the storehouse of God and retrieved the solution. Doesn't it make sense to bring this often unconscious process into the world of the conscious mind and your daily activities?

By creating a peaceful inner environment and opening yourself up to inspiration, you lay the groundwork for your seed thought to come into awareness and lead you to fulfillment.

Your Seed Thought and Business

Since your seed thought contains the nucleus of your mission in the world, it plays a central role in creating the business venture best suited to your talents. The definitive thought behind your business is crucial to its success or failure. Your seed thought is of paramount importance.

Many people assume that business success is solely the result of raising sufficient capital and working hard. They do not believe that the concept for a business can be developed while sitting in a chair or taking a walk on a beach; but that is exactly how many successful businesses were initially created. When we are relaxed and receptive—when we are *being* rather than *doing*—we receive so much more!

The story behind the creation of the business seed thought for Richard Fishman, *The Prosperity Game's* co-author, demonstrates these principles. Richard said, "Before I started my real estate investment business, I met with my prospective business partner, Brian. We spent a wonderful morning at the Claremont Hotel in Berkeley talking about our vision. How many apartment buildings did we want to own? Who would do what? What would our business philosophy be?

"The meeting was so powerful that even years later, we referred back to those few hours. That time was a marker for us, the reference point for our seed thought. Whenever we felt that we were drifting off course from our original vision, we would say, 'Remember the Claremont.' This phrase brought us back to where we needed to be—in the presence of the seed thought behind our business.

"During that initial brainstorming session, Brian and I succeeded in distilling our business vision down to one succinct phrase: 'Maximize revenue through tenant satisfaction.' Our business would provide a great product and we trusted that tenants would be willing to pay a good price for it. We would have to be on our game and operate to their satisfaction, or they would not be amenable to living in our communities. If we were successful, we would positively impact the lives of thousands of tenants and their families, as well as our employees. Our business was built on the bedrock of our spiritual beliefs. We would serve others first and believed that we would be rewarded for doing so. And we were!"

For those who are still wondering what a great seed thought looks like, we took the liberty of coming up with a few examples based on the achievements of certain well-known individuals.

Mary Kay Ash—Bringing opportunity to women
William Gates III—A personal computer on every desk

John Rockefeller—Cheap oil for everyone
Will Keith Kellogg—Nutritious cereal for breakfast
Thomas Edison—Electricity in everyone's home
Oprah Winfrey—Live your best life
Henry Ford—A car for every working man
Walt Disney—Making families smile
Howard Schultz (CEO of Starbucks)—A neighborly place
    for great coffee
Tom Monaghan (founder of Domino's) —A warm pizza in
    30 minutes

Each of these women and men devoted their lives to making one simple idea blossom. Their achievement arose from their ability to concentrate all of their energies on manifesting one vision—a single seed thought.

Initially, some of the most successful seed thoughts provided no clue to the great success and tremendous wealth that would result from their implementation. When Bill Gates worked with IBM to develop an operating system for personal computers, no one could foresee that one day ordinary folks would want to spend hours every day in front of a computer. However, Gates sensed that personal computers had the potential to replace the large mainframe computers then in use by many businesses, and he pursued his idea.

Among the seed thoughts of the people we interviewed for this book are the following:

Kim Gay—Provide cost-effective products to long-term
    care facilities
Scott Walker—Help people feel better quickly through a
    multi-modality healing technique

Patty DeDominic—Provide professional staff dedicated to
quality

Stephen Crisman—Make documentary films that enhance
and improve people's lives

Carl Terzian—Transform public relations into a secular
ministry

Reading and reflecting upon the ideas contained in this
book will help you become more receptive to receiving your seed
thought. Over the days and weeks ahead, *attune within to receive
the seed thought that is right for you.*

How to Find Your Seed Thought

The key to finding your seed thought is to go within, to your
center—the place where your soul resides, the essence of who you
are. Your soulful center holds the real truth about you in its purest
form. It is where you know the essential purpose of your life. For
many people, this place is their heart, where they feel passion for
life and their connection to God.

You do not need to reinvent the wheel. Over the centuries,
people have developed a variety of techniques for internalizing
their consciousness. Certain methods work well for many people,
but not for everyone. Therefore, it's best to find an approach that
appeals to you, and make it your own. When you connect with
your essential nature, it will change your life.

Certain techniques have proven effective for many people in
preparing the soil of their being to receive and nurture a seed
thought. Among these time-honored techniques are prayer,
meditation, and walking in nature. Perhaps you like going to
the beach, prefer a walk in the woods, or find inspiration in a
stroll through the city. Another tool is visualization; whether self-

created or guided by another, either personally present or through a recording.

Once you are centered in your soul, it is time to connect with the Divine. Johannes Brahms attuned with God by going deep within and asking Him questions. Those questions were: "Where have I come from?" "Who am I?" "Where am I going?" Many others have had success by asking similar questions. If these particular questions don't appeal to you, create your own.

You can also use affirmations to attune with Divinty. Among the affirmations you might want to consider are:

I am one with the ocean of life.

I am free to do what God wants.

My heart expands to feel God's will for me.

I embrace my divine destiny.

If none of these affirmations work for you, use one from another source or create a phrase that really moves you.

After you reach out to the Divine, relax. How do you relax and become receptive? Some people like to listen to soft instrumental music. Others like to become involved in creative endeavors. Get out some drawing pencils or crayons and sketch, paint, sculpt, or throw pottery. Any pastime that opens you up will work.

After he parted ways with Sigmund Freud, the famous Swiss psychologist Carl Jung entered a period of inner uncertainty. During this "state of disorientation," Carl Jung twice reviewed the details of his entire life to try to determine what might be the cause of the disturbance, but this investigation led to nothing but a fresh acknowledgment of his own ignorance.[9]

Carl Jung then said to himself, "Since I know nothing at all, I shall simply do whatever occurs to me." He consciously submitted to the impulses of his unconscious. The first thing that came to the surface was a childhood memory from his tenth or eleventh year. During that period Carl Jung had passionately played with building blocks, creating little houses and castles.

To his astonishment, this memory was accompanied by a good deal of emotion. Carl Jung said to himself, "There is still life in these things. The small boy is still around and possesses a creative life which I lack. But how can I make my way to it?" He wanted to reestablish contact with that time of creativity and felt he needed to take up once more the child's life with his childish games. "This moment was a turning point in my fate, but I gave in only after endless resistances and with a sense of resignation." Carl Jung spent hours playing with stones, building cottages, a castle, a whole village.[10]

Explore the world of your dreams. Keep a journal beside your bed and write down your nocturnal adventures. They may hold the key to your divine destiny.

If you are not a dreamer or able to throw yourself into fantasy, take a linear approach. Reflect upon your life. Write down your ten most enjoyable achievements. Any activity that instills in you a deep sense of well-being, resonates in your bones, or fills you with peace and joy, is likely related to your seed thought.

Your answer could appear in many different guises and might come all at once—or gradually over a long period of time. It may manifest itself as a picture in your mind, or perhaps a sweet inner voice will speak to you. You may have an intuitive flash of understanding, or a gut-level feeling. Or the message may come from an external source—a phrase that grabs your attention while reading a book, a wisp of conversation with a friend, or a line in a movie.

You may not fully understand your answer when it appears and only fully comprehend its meaning over a period of time. You may not receive a direct response at all, but simply notice opportunities that arise. This heightened awareness is another way in which the Divine reveals itself.

Those of a more analytical bent will appreciate the familiar phrase, "Luck is where opportunity meets preparation;" or, as Louis Pasteur said, "Luck favors the prepared mind." Many of our interviewees live by the maxim *carpe diem*—seize the day. They notice things that others might miss, including potential opportunities. Those opportunities become seed thoughts, and successful people take action on their seed thoughts to turn them into reality.

Kim Gay is the founder and former owner of Associated Provider Services Inc., a specialty medical equipment company. For a number of years after its creation, Associated Provider Services experienced double-digit growth annually, and the company had revenue of $3.5 million in 2006. In September 2007, Kim sold her company to Recovercare LLC, a national medical equipment company located in Radnor, Pennsylvania.

Prior to creating Associated Provider Services, Kim worked for a medical equipment manufacturer. She had risen from sales representative to national sales manager, and although Kim loved healthcare in general—and particularly the specialty medical equipment segment of the industry—she knew there was no likelihood of further promotion.

Kim began looking for opportunities. She discovered that the national medical equipment suppliers had no interest in providing products to rural long-term care facilities in her home state of Georgia. Kim did additional research and determined there was a huge untapped market in these rural areas for specialized medical beds. While a hospital would need these beds for an average of only three to five days per patient, a long-term care facility would require the same beds for an average of forty-five days per patient.

Kim knew that *this* was her opportunity, and it became her seed thought. Years of experience with these products had prepared Kim for the task of successfully growing her seed thought into a prosperous business.

Vrajesh Lal is the president and principal shareholder of Just For Wraps, Inc., a clothing company. He started the business with $800. It took seven years for the company to hit the million-dollar revenue mark, and another seven years for the company to grow to $20 million in annual sales. In 2007, the company did about $65 million in sales. In addition to Just For Wraps, Inc., Vrajesh Lal has several investments in real estate and securities in the United States and India.

Vrajesh was born and raised in India. During his childhood, he was enamored with the many saintly figures who visited his home. A saintly person tutored him in physics during exams. Vrajesh also admired his cousin, who fresh out of college obtained a job at IBM that paid one thousand rupees per month at a time when most Indians were making just three hundred. Vrajesh wanted to attain success—both spiritually and in the material world.

Vrajesh Lal believes that you should keep your door open so that opportunity doesn't have to knock, it simply comes right in . He had always wanted to give business a try. While serving as an assistant to the dean of the University of Southern California

School of Business, Vrajesh was asked to help an apparel importer/ retailer review their financial statements and operations.

The company directly imported clothing from India and Indonesia for its four retail stores in Laguna Beach. However, there were many problems with this method of doing business. The turnaround time for apparel from India was four to five months. Deliveries were late, there was a high rejection rate and everything that could go wrong did go wrong.

It was obvious to Vrajesh that there had to be a better way to run this business. Although it cost twice as much to make clothing in the U.S. as compared to India and Indonesia, by doing so he could control the manufacturing process from beginning to end and eliminate many of the problems experienced by the importer. Vrajesh believed that he could turn out better quality products with a faster turnaround time by producing clothing in the U.S. This idea became his seed thought.

Edna Hennessee's seed thought arrived in a prosaic, practical manner. She perceived a need and created a product to meet that need. Edna was the founder and sole owner of Cosmetic Specialty Labs in Lawton, Oklahoma. Cosmetic Specialty Labs is a private-label manufacturing facility that grows, processes, formulates, manufactures, packages, and ships aloe vera based products for more than 9,500 customers in the United States and thirty other countries.

Edna started her journey to success as a nurse, eventually opening a beauty salon. Her beauty business began with one operator and expanded to become a forty-operator beauty shop. As her business grew, Edna found it difficult to attract employees who were properly trained. The solution was clear: She needed to open her own beauty college. And so she did! This results-oriented approach arose naturally from Edna's belief that you should either do things right or not do them at all.

Along the way, Edna began producing her own beauty products to replace the commercially available products, which were not up to her high standards. Due to her training as a nurse, Edna focused on the medicinal rather than cosmetic attributes of skincare. She wanted to do beauty products right.

Edna was particularly passionate about helping people with bad complexions. This was a result of her suffering in high school due to a bad complexion. She understood from personal experience how much pain this can cause, and wanted to help others avoid the distress she endured. Edna searched far and wide for a product that would work with acne. When she realized that none of the available products would meet her needs, Edna created her own aloe vera based acne products. Soon she was producing a complete line of aloe vera based skincare products.

The fame of her skincare products spread, and a company in Dallas asked Edna to produce a line of aloe vera based cosmetics for them. Shortly thereafter, five other companies requested that Edna create aloe vera cosmetic lines and she opened Cosmetic Specialty Labs.

In chapter 1 we promised to provide you with the details of Zachary Taylor's seed thought incubation process. Zachary is the creative genius who designed and built the Luxor Sky Beam atop the Luxor Hotel and Casino in Las Vegas. That beam, as built, emits an astonishing 36 billion candlepower, making it the world's brightest light.[11]

When he was a teenager, Zachary had the desire to enhance the experience of audiences at live musical events by producing lighting and other special effects. He developed a technique for consciously turning this thought into reality. Zachary focused his attention on this concert-enhancement idea, to give it additional gravity. With the added weight, this supersaturated concept sank into his subconscious mind, where it gestated for a period of time. Whenever the thought flashed before his conscious mind, Zachary would meditate on it. Eventually the idea gained sufficient form and clarity to rise from his subconscious mind into his conscious mind as he came out of meditation. Zachary then committed the concept to paper and began producing musical events.

Zachary now uses this seed thought incubation process for each of his creative projects. You might be thinking about now, "This all sounds a bit technical—even theoretical. Does this process really work?" Let's explore how it worked for Zachary Taylor.

Zachary began producing lighting and other special effects for dances at National Guard armories at the age of 18. As time passed, he produced shows at ever-larger venues including civic auditoriums, arenas, and stadiums. He staged special effects lighting on two national tours for the Who, and created show elements for many other major artists, including the Moody Blues, Neil Diamond, Barry Manilow, and Journey. Additional clients for whom Zachary has produced lighting and special effects include the Olympics, Disneyland, the Pan American Games, the California State Lottery and the U.S. Department of the Interior.

Let's review Zachary's seed thought incubation process in a step-by-step fashion. When Zachary experiences a flash of inspiration, an idea he would like to pursue, he infuses it with his desire to bring it to fruition. He also concentrates on the thought, thereby giving it mental strength. Adding emotional and mental energy to the idea gives it more weight, more gravity. The thought becomes self-contained and develops its own persona.

This crystallized, supersaturated concept then sinks into Zachary's subconscious mind. The work of transforming this thought into a clear concept takes place in his subconscious. Zachary gives the idea time to settle, to develop a life of its own, to network with other ideas. Occasionally the thought will come to him while he is dreaming and he will work with it there.

From time to time, Zachary will become aware of the thought while he is in a conscious state. When this happens, he knows it is calling for attention. He will give the concept some time to take form by clearing his mind and focusing on the idea. During this meditation, he deepens his connection with the idea and integrates with it.

The process of developing a concept is similar to approaching a destination. When you come closer to a destination, it becomes larger and larger until you eventually arrive. A thought also becomes clearer and clearer over time. You can see what the idea was and what it is developing into. As you meditate upon the thought, you bring nutrients to it from the conscious world. The length of time for the process varies from idea to idea. The more profound or expansive the concept is, the longer it takes to develop.

After a number of meditations, Zachary merges so deeply with the thought that he and the thought become one. The concept has matured with sufficient form and clarity to stand on its own in the world. Before, it was merely a thought form, now it is fully defined and very specific. This is similar to a chick developing inside an egg and gaining enough maturity to break out of its shell or a butterfly emerging from its cocoon, spreading its wings, rising into the air and taking flight.

The mature idea rises from Zachary's subconscious mind into his conscious mind as he emerges from meditation. It bursts out in a torrent, because the thought has been fully formulated within. Zachary commits the concept to paper, outlines the project, and develops its components.

A concrete example will help you understand how this process unfolds. After working with high-intensity lighting and applying color to it for a project, Zachary had the thought that it would be nice to create a rainbow. At that point the rainbow was just an idea—he did not actually know how to achieve this result. Undaunted, Zachary asserted to himself, "I'm going to figure out how and where to do this."

Zachary then considered several different kinds of lighting instruments. He thought about the capabilities of each, and what he could do with them. Zachary's desire and concentrated mental focus wrapped around the rainbow concept and locked it into a self-contained, crystallized form, which dropped into his subconscious mind. Over time the thought developed a life of its own in his subconscious mind.

Zachary meditated on the rainbow whenever he felt called to do so. Eventually the rainbow was mature enough to stand on its own. It had become clearly defined and very specific. This fully formed idea filled his conscious mind after Zachary came out of his next "rainbow meditation." He knew it was time to commit the rainbow concept to paper. The plan materialized fully formed and Zachary developed the components necessary to complete the project, including a venue in which to create his rainbow of light. Zachary Taylor created two half-mile-long rainbows over Disneyland for its 30th anniversary.

The subconscious is the source of your creative power and you can directly access that power by tapping into the subconscious mind. If Zachary's seed thought incubation process does not appeal to you, there is a simpler approach you might want to try. This method has been recommended by hypnotherapists for years. Before you go to sleep at night, turn your nascent seed thought into a symbol, a metaphor, a story, or imagery. This is the language of the subconscious mind. Make this creation the last thought you have before you fall asleep. Then pay attention to the new thoughts and ideas that arise over the next few days. These are the fruits born from your subconscious mind as it shapes your seed thought.

The first step in discovering your seed thought is to find your center through prayer, meditation, a walk in nature, visualization, or other means that help you become still within. "Be still and know that I am God." (Psalms 46:10) From this clear state of being—this spiritually inspired place—quietly ask questions, repeat affirmations, or communicate your request to the Divine in whatever way works best for you. The final step is to relax and be open to receive.

You may find it useful to create art, explore your dreams, or take an analytical approach in order to increase your receptivity. If it appeals to you, use Zachary Taylor's seed thought incubation process, or work on developing your seed thought in your subconscious mind while you are dreaming.

Once you receive your seed thought, there are additional steps to take to ensure it is both practical and appropriate for you.

Write Down Your Seed Thought and Test It

Remember the meeting Richard had with Brian at the Claremont Hotel when they developed the seed thought for their real estate business? While reflecting upon that day, Richard said, "We wrote down our game plan and, to this day, I wonder if any of it would have materialized if we had not done so."

Although the great majority of people do not write down their goals, a few do. Those few who put their goals on paper have been found to be much more successful than people who do not. A study at Dominican University, *Summary of Recent Goals Research,* by Gail Matthews, Ph.D., validated the effectiveness of written goals.

Write your seed thought down when it first comes to you, even if you have to stop everything else to do so.

Great people manifest great things by acting on their ideas. Writing down your seed thought is a good first step toward bringing it into manifestation. It is all about taking action. Keep refining your initial seed thought until it expresses in just a few words everything you want to accomplish. The more you refine it, the clearer your direction will be. Then, like a magnifying glass focusing the sun's rays, your seed thought will so focus your dreams that they become an all-consuming fire.

Richard's vocational path in life is an example of how a seed thought may take years to bring forth fruit. Richard said, "As a young man, I had a deep fascination with buildings and real estate, and dreamed of becoming a real estate investor. My first job out of college was helping a nonprofit organization rehabilitate apartment buildings, followed by a position in the housing program of a city government. When I moved to California, I took a job with a mortgage company. Since I was good at math and this job connected me to the world of buildings and real estate, I felt I was moving closer to my dream.

"When I opened my own mortgage company, the thought persisted that I should be investing in real estate. I often complained to God that I was not doing what I wanted to do. While my impatience was understandable, the jobs I had perceived as detours were a necessary part of the path to my goal. Through my various jobs, God provided me with the tools I needed to fully develop my seed thought and become truly prosperous.

"After fifteen years in the mortgage business, I began buying investment real estate. If I had not learned about finance at the mortgage company and the practicalities of owning real estate from my clients, I would not have been nearly as successful."

The moral of Richard's story is to be patient with God, Who knows exactly what you need and when you need it in order to manifest your seed thought properly. If you don't fight against what is, you will have a much smoother ride.

Once you have received your seed thought, thoroughly test it. Determine whether you can create a business based upon this idea that is in accord with your spiritual beliefs and practices. Are you comfortable with what will be required of you? If your seed thought is fully aligned with your highest aspirations, it has passed this test. However, if at any point your seed thought does not resonate with your spirituality, either find a way to bring it into alignment or seek another seed thought.

Carl Terzian created a full-service public relations firm which is fully aligned with his personal beliefs. Carl Terzian Associates has assisted more than 5,000 companies and individuals with corporate, crisis, executive, philanthropic and institutional public relations and marketing. Carl's client list is a veritable *Who's Who* of national and local corporations, including: ABC Television, Bank of America, the California Chamber of Commerce, the *Los Angeles Times*, Northwestern Mutual Life Insurance Company, the Southern California Association of Governments, *The Wall Street Journal*, and Yamaha Motor Corporation, U.S.A.

In college, Carl was trained in political science and considered pursuing several different career options, including politics, education, and the ministry. He also had an interest in serving the nonprofit community. Carl asked God for help in finding the best use of his talents and in 1969 was led to combine all of these interests by creating his public relations firm.

Carl's vision led to a unique approach in helping his clients— through facilitating eight hundred networking events each year. Guests are personally selected by Carl from the business, nonprofit, public, and professional sectors. Through these events, the nonprofit leaders in attendance gain exposure to people they wouldn't normally connect with, and in turn, his clients find fulfillment through supporting nonprofit organizations. Carl said "Traditional PR wasn't interesting to me. Public relations was a vehicle by which I and others could give back." Part of that giving back is accomplished through Carl placing more than five hundred people on nonprofit boards each year.

In doing business, it usually comes down to who you know—and Carl Terzian is a master at building relationships. Carl Terzian Associates takes its clients out into the community to meet people. Carl teaches his clients how to build lasting connections and feels that God has blessed and ordained his secular ministry.

Mark Myers is a senior housing expert and real estate broker with Marcus & Millichap in Chicago, Illinois. During the past fifteen years, Mark has sold over $2 billion of commercial property in forty-three states, from the East Coast to the West Coast. Of those sales, a little over $1.5 billion have been senior housing, including the January 2007 sale of 26 assisted living facilities in 11 states for $190 million, as well as the August 2011 sale of 6 retirement campuses in Indiana for $123 Million, representing two of his largest transactions to date.

Mark represents the sellers of senior housing facilities throughout the U.S. This business fits well with his personal beliefs because it has the right mixture of elements. Mark is a "super servant" and he solves problems for people who really need his services. It is also a way to make a lot of money, honestly and ethically.

Mark spends his entire day helping people meet their needs. Many mom-and-pop senior housing property owners are extremely unsophisticated about the issues that are relevant to buying and selling businesses. These people need and greatly benefit from

Mark's analytical and people skills. He connects the unconnected by bringing in buyers from across the country for rural properties, in addition to regional and local buyers. This creates a pool of competing bidders. Serving others in this manner is totally in alignment with Mark's world view.

Kim Gay has a very similar story. One of her core beliefs is if you help others and provide needed services, everything else will fall into place. You simply need to know who your customers are and what they need. Then you go the extra mile—spending whatever time is necessary to take care of your customers. Kim did some research and it touched her heart when she found that the elderly and disabled in long-term care facilities were not receiving the same level of service as others. The business she ultimately decided to start provided the opportunity to live her beliefs by providing services to the elderly and disabled—people who truly needed them.

We would ask that you bear in mind an important caveat with regard to this ethical vetting process. Often seed thoughts do not bear fruit for sincere people due to conscious, subconscious, or unconscious conflicts. Make certain that your own limiting beliefs do not restrict your seed thought.

For example, many spiritual aspirants believe—consciously, subconsciously, or unconsciously—that making a profit is against God's laws. Such people often lead a life of financial minimization. If this lifestyle comes from a true desire for voluntary simplicity, it may be an appropriate choice.

However, when this lifestyle arises from a belief that money is the root of all evil, it is simply a convenient excuse for hiding from the world. Wealth is neither good nor evil.

"Money is the root of all evil" is only a partial rendering of a biblical passage, and, as a consequence, misconstrues the Divine message. The complete quote is "The love of money is the root of all evil." (1 Timothy 6:10)

There is nothing wrong with having money or making a profit. You are made in God's image and abundance is available to you. The Bhagavad-Gita states that those who perform material duties to further their own development are heavenly messengers inviting lost souls back to God's mansion of joy.

After your seed thought passes the ethical sniff test, you must ascertain whether it is practical for you to pursue this business idea. Does it fit with your other responsibilities?

When one duty conflicts with another, something has to give. If you realize that starting a business is not going to work with raising your children, you have discovered a great truth and need to act accordingly. You cannot be "all things to all men."

You also need to determine whether implementing a particular business idea makes sense in terms of who you are and the skills you possess. Ask yourself, "Are my ambitions in alignment with my abilities?" Take personality and aptitude tests, speak with those who know you well and interview people who are in that business. Through this process you will determine whether it makes sense from a logical standpoint for you to begin this endeavor. This self-analysis is an extremely important step in establishing a secure foundation for your new business.

Below are some examples of potential seed thoughts and the results of passing them through this ethical and practical testing process.

Cheap cigarettes for Third World children (morally repugnant)
Using gravity to power automobiles (beam me up Scotty)
Growing bananas in Alaska (not feasible)

Owning a chain of environmentally friendly dry cleaners (maybe, depending on your skill set)

Once your seed thought has passed the ethical and practical tests, you are ready to progress to the second step of the process. It is now time to determine whether this seed thought is your calling.

STEP TWO – DETERMINE AND ACCEPT YOUR CALLING

CHAPTER 3

Okay, so you have this great idea that fills you with enthusiasm and energy. You have confirmed that the idea fits with your world view and is practical. Yet, how do you know if your seed thought is your calling? Is this idea, out of all the ideas out there, the one for you to pursue?

Drake Sadler is the cofounder, chairman of the board, and single largest shareholder of Traditional Medicinals herbal tea company. Since its inception, Traditional Medicinals has been wildly successful, and it is one of the largest and fastest growing herbal tea companies in America. The company uses only the highest quality pharmacopoeial-grade herbs. Well over a billion bags of tea have been produced at their facility in Sebastopol, California.

In early 1974, Drake and two friends created the vision for Traditional Medicinals in the storeroom of a small herb shop on the Russian River in Northern California. Their goal was to provide the finest quality herbal teas for self-care, while preserving the knowledge and herbal formulas of traditional herbal medicine.

When the opportunity arose to begin creating herbal teas, Drake already owned several businesses. He was stretched to the limit and wasn't certain he should pursue a new business prospect. Drake realized he needed to concentrate on growing one business, but which one?

Rather than plotting a course of action based solely upon an analysis of the potential for each business, Drake sought clarity through a spiritual retreat. During his retreat, he prayed to God for guidance. Although Drake continued to pray until exhausted, no answer came.

Drake returned to Northern California and began working on business plans for each company to see if that would bring him greater clarity. Two weeks later there was a huge fire in the Russian River area. All of Drake's businesses except the herb company burned to the ground. Drake had received a sudden and dramatic answer from God. His calling was clear.

Others realize their calling over a longer period of time. Kim Gay knew there was no likelihood of promotion with her employer so she began to look around for business opportunities. It made sense to Kim to remain in the specialty medical equipment industry, since she knew it well. Kim discovered that the national medical equipment suppliers had no interest in providing products to rural long-term care facilities in her home state of Georgia, even though they actively pursued this market in metropolitan Atlanta. She conducted research, determined that the potential market was substantial and decided to pursue this business.

When Kim began working on her business, synchronistic events happened over and over again. She needed a reasonably priced medical bed, and the day she had that thought, the perfect bed magically appeared. On her first day in business, Kim landed a small company as her initial client, which helped her gain experience and develop operational systems. At that point, Kim knew she had discovered her calling.

Through a series of fortuitous events occurring over a period of time, Kim Gay's calling became clear. Drake Sadler's calling announced itself by literally burning up all of his other businesses. Its arrival was sudden and left no doubt, although it appeared in response to an intense period of soul-searching and entreaties to God for guidance.

You can't help but love Drake's experience, where the heavens opened to reveal his true calling. While such an event makes for an exciting and engaging story, not everyone is blessed with such a dramatic response. Your calling may reveal itself to you more slowly and incrementally, wrestled from the school of life through trial and error. Yet the results are no less striking, as you will see through the tale of Mark Myers' path to his calling.

Our story opens in 1990. Mark was a full-time employee of Group 1 Investments, a small Chicago real estate syndicator, and spent his days overseeing the management of Class B and C apartment communities in the Midwest. He also burned the midnight oil—often until 2:00 a.m.—completing coursework for his MBA degree.

While his business school classmates at Northwestern University dreamed of life as corporate bigwigs, Mark had a different vision. He longed to be the master of his own destiny. Mark would become an entrepreneur, with no one to answer to but himself. Yet he was also practical and keenly aware that he had absolutely no experience in running a business.

With graduation drawing nigh, Mark was caught on the horns of this dilemma. How could he find a business opportunity that gave him the freedom he yearned for while also providing a safety net and a roadmap to success? Then he hit upon a strategy that seemed to fulfill all of his aspirations and address all of his concerns: he would purchase a franchise.

In 1991, filled with exuberance from success in graduate school, Mark sought a franchise within which to apply his newfound knowledge. His wife, Karen, reluctantly agreed with this plunge into the entrepreneurial world. Their search through the franchise jungle led them to Blimpie, the chain of sub sandwich shops. Mark was impressed with their proven track record and huge East Coast presence.

Mark was not completely naïve and investigated this opportunity prior to taking the leap. He contacted several franchisees, who reported mixed results. Some attested to their personal success with Blimpie, while others reported they hadn't done so well. Mark chose to focus on the good news and discounted the bad.

He reasoned that the unhappy owners were ineffective or inexperienced entrepreneurs, or simply failed to follow the Blimpie business formula. Surely Mark would do much better, with his real estate syndication background and degree from one of the most prestigious MBA programs in the country. In fact, Mark was so taken with the idea of being one of the first Blimpie franchisees in Chicago that he bought not one, but three franchises!

Shortly thereafter, Mark and Karen found their first location—a great 2,000-square-foot restaurant space in a heavily trafficked suburb Northwest of Chicago. After burning through $60,000 in renovations, Mark became aware of warning signs. A franchisee in the Chicago region sold his Blimpie store. Mark was stunned. Just a few months earlier, that very franchisee had regaled him with tales of success.

Mark knew he had to get to the bottom of the story. He contacted the man and the sad truth surfaced. The former Blimpie owner admitted that his franchise had actually been performing poorly, but he felt he needed to encourage Mark to join him. The man had reasoned that additional Blimpie franchises in the area would create a critical mass, propelling his own business to profitability. He had lied to Mark, thinking it would save his own skin. That phone call taught Mark a valuable lesson. Always thoroughly investigate any business deal in advance, carefully review the books and records of the business and never completely rely on or disregard any of the information you discover.

From the outset, Karen had been a reluctant co-entrepreneur. She told Mark, "People don't graduate from the number one business school in the country and then open a sandwich shop. You need to utilize the great education you received." Mark had ignored her sage advice, just as he had disregarded the warnings from the unsuccessful Blimpie franchisees.

After the phone conversation with the former Blimpie shop owner, Mark knew his wife was right. He had spent their nest egg on a bad idea. They were in deep trouble and the restaurant had to go. Yet, Mark knew that the only way out was to open the restaurant and run it for a while before selling it. After all, who was going to buy a half-baked idea? Mark and Karen ran their Blimpie franchise for seven months. Fortunately, both had kept their full-time jobs.

The Blimpie experience was the low point in Mark's life. Here he was, the take charge MBA, behind a counter making turkey and provolone sandwiches. Marketing the business made Mark feel even worse. Blimpie had a bear mascot costume that franchisees could have someone wear on the sidewalk near the store to attract drive-by traffic. Mark vividly remembers standing in front of his Blimpie in the bear costume, begging for business, to no avail.

Worst of all was the experience of having teenagers drive by in their rusted out jalopies, flipping him off and cursing at him.

Mark had a master's degree in management from a prestigious business school and couldn't even run one little sandwich shop. He felt humiliated and had hit rock bottom. His family's entire nest egg of $120,000 (a total of $90,000 to complete the renovations plus $30,000 on operating losses during the 7 months of operation) was invested in this franchise. When they managed to sell the franchise it was a hollow victory—their $120,000 investment returned a paltry $20,000.

In business, as in all aspects of life, hard lessons often lead to great wisdom. This seeming failure brought Mark new insights. He determined that the experience would not define his life. Mark thought to himself, "I am a child of God, a husband to my wife, and we are a family. Personal relationships are more important than any business, whether it succeeds or fails. Plus, I now know that my wife and my God love me unconditionally, despite my blind spots and foibles. I have lost everything but am actually a rich man!"

His new perspective gave Mark a stronger inner foundation, and he became more objective about himself. He no longer overestimated his own abilities. Receptivity became his ally, and Mark began to listen to what life was saying. He paid closer attention to how it was directing him, and relied upon the guidance, support, and strength he received through his relationship with God and his family. The lessons were brutal for this brash young man who struck out on his own, heedless of the advice of others. Yet, through the crucible of this difficult experience, Mark gained greater understanding about life and himself.

Mark brought this increased receptivity and deeper understanding to his real estate career, and became aware of things he had not previously noticed. During this time of struggle, the real estate firm for whom he was working purchased two apartment properties in Denton and Richardson, Texas. The broker for the transaction pocketed $100,000—more than twice as much as Mark's annual salary of around $40,000. Mark thought to himself, I can do this and this is what I want to do. Through doing research, he discovered that the average real estate agent with two years experience in the Chicago office of Marcus & Millichap, a national income property broker, earned $200,000 per year.

Mark told Karen of his interest in joining Marcus & Millichap as a commercial property broker. "If I can stick around for two years," Mark said, "I can make a good living using the real estate skills I have already developed."

Karen replied, "At least this is closer to what you were trained for, and you can utilize your education and background." Karen did admonish Mark, saying, "If this fails, you need to get a *real* job."

Mark interviewed for a real estate broker position at Marcus & Millichap and got the job. That was eighteen years ago, and he has never needed to consider that real job.

At Marcus & Millichap, Mark started at the bottom, selling apartment buildings in the lowest income areas of the far western suburb of Aurora. Not surprisingly, he found it very difficult to convince investors to purchase these properties. After a year, Mark approached his boss, Linwood Thompson, to strategize about more effective ways to sell Aurora apartment buildings. As fate would have it, Linwood was talking on the phone with Lee Harris, who was in charge of the senior housing group for Marcus & Millichap.

When Linwood finished the call, he asked if Mark would like to develop the Chicago area senior housing group for Lee. Mark remembered the advice he had received from his former employer, Howard Wolkoff of Group 1 Investments: "The key to becoming a successful broker is to specialize. The more specialized knowledge you have, the more valuable you are to the buying community." Mark immediately said "yes" to this interesting opportunity.

Mark did not yet realize this was his calling. He simply knew that he could add value to real estate transactions by developing specialized knowledge. When Mark immersed himself in the senior housing market, he realized that the owners of senior housing facilities had a great need for professional representation. They often owned a single facility that was thirty or forty years old, were now elderly themselves, wanted to retire and had no viable succession plan - either they had no children or their children had no desire to be in that business.

At that time, there was no methodology for valuation of senior housing facilities. The owners of these facilities were not connected to the capital markets or to the bigger buyers. As a consequence, the sellers relied on a very limited pool of potential local buyers. These factors made it difficult to sell and finance such properties. Mark saw a tremendous opportunity to serve these owners by creating a much larger market for their senior housing facilities. Mark also saw the hand of God here, presenting him with an opportunity to use his life experience and skills to help these owners.

His trials and tribulations with Blimpie gave Mark a keen appreciation for the role of personal relationships in business affairs. He understood that these sellers were not sophisticated business people and they would need to be approached with a soft bedside manner.

This industry also required the skills Mark had developed in business school and through working with real estate. The purchase and sale agreements for senior housing facilities are very long and complex. This is due to the fact that the buyer is purchasing an ongoing, highly regulated business in addition to commercial real estate. Mark's analytical, marketing and negotiating skills would be required in valuing each long-term care facility and in finding and dealing with the buyers. Initially, Mark sold both senior housing and apartment properties. For the past fifteen years, he has exclusively sold senior housing.

Mark developed a step-by-step approach for serving the owners of senior care facilities. He interviews potential clients to learn the story behind their business and their goals for the future. Mark also determines how best to help them realize their dreams. He offers a unique service and does a good job for his sellers.

This business was the right mixture for Mark. By making money honestly and ethically while utilizing his talents in performing a service for people, Mark could be a "super servant" and help them solve their problems. All of the other jobs Mark ever had felt like a chore, but selling senior housing is his passion and pleasure. This work makes Mark feels spiritually alive and morally good. Over time, he came to the realization that this was his calling.

Receptivity is the key for all of us in both finding our seed thought and determining whether our seed thought is our calling. Mark was no exception. He believed he had found his calling when he became a Blimpie franchisee, but the results speak for themselves. As a result, Mark became more attuned to the messages being presented through his life experience.

Through increased receptivity, Mark received a seed thought—selling real estate—which was refined through business experience into selling senior housing. Over time, he realized that this seed thought was his calling. Mark's experience demonstrates one path to your calling: open up, trust, pay attention, and heed the good advice that comes your way.

What is a Calling?

Within you is a desire to find meaning and purpose in life. It is this desire that drives you to seek out your role, to find your calling in life. Being human means making the most of all the gifts that have been given to you.

The first step in discovering your calling is to center within and be still—be receptive to the Divine inspiration. "Behold, I stand at the door and knock: if any man hear my voice and open the door, I will come in to him and will sup with him and he with me." (Revelations 3:20)

You don't need to lie awake at night worrying about your calling. Your calling may be what you are doing right now. It lays not so much in what you do as in how you do it.

Sometimes we are pulled away from our calling by belief systems. Stephen Crisman is a well-respected documentary filmmaker. He always knew that he was called to make films. Creating and filming engaging, enlightening stories is what Stephen loves to do and he is very good at it. His films have received seven Emmy nominations and he has won an Emmy.

Long ago, however, Stephen was diverted from his calling. He had just married and felt the proverbial wolf at the door that often seems to stand between people and their calling. So Stephen did what many do. He took the road to financial security first. Stephen became manager of the first Hard Rock Café when it opened in London; and he opened the second Hard Rock Café in New York.

Stephen left the Hard Rock Café organization to start his own restaurant, Sam's Café. Again Stephen was successful and he grew Sam's Café into a chain of eight restaurants. Stephen ultimately sold the chain and created another brand of restaurants. Success begets success.

Yet all along, Stephen experienced the pull of his true calling. He felt something was missing in the midst of all this activity and financial success. When Stephen sold his second chain of restaurants, he vowed to heed his calling. He would become what he was always meant to be—a documentary filmmaker.

There is, of course, a great irony in Stephen Crisman's story. He waited to follow his calling until he was financially secure. Yet, Stephen's calling has provided substantial income.

Connecting with your soul opens up a well of energy within you. The ancient Greeks called this enthusiasm, literally "being possessed by God." Having a calling helps people become successful because it brings with it a virtually unlimited flow of energy. You'll need that energy to get started and to overcome obstacles along the way.

Chiropractor Scott Walker experienced this tremendous energy that pours through you when you make your seed thought your calling. Scott created the Neuro Emotional Technique ("NET"), a unique mind/body approach to health care which combines elements from several healing arts, including psychology, acupuncture, and chiropractic. Scott now teaches NET to healthcare professionals throughout the world.

While he was creating NET and its related training seminars, Scott felt the incredible wellspring of energy that gushes forth when you experience your calling. Looking back on that period of time, Scott said "It was like I felt a pushing force from the back and a pulling force from the front. So I guess you could say that I was driven from behind and pulled from the front, but the bottom line is it felt effortless and I felt like I was on a fun ride. " He would go to bed late in the evening and get up at 2:00 or 3:00 a.m. Even though Scott managed only four hours of sleep a night, he was never tired. Scott said, "The whole process felt effortless. All I had to do was open my eyes, get out of bed, and the energy was there."

The more you open yourself to receive input and guidance from within, the more the Divine will participate in your life and the greater will be your good fortune. "If God be for us, who can be against us? [S]hall He not ... also freely give us all things?" (Romans 8:31-32)

Please don't misunderstand. Finding and accepting your calling doesn't automatically mean your life is going to be free and easy. Even the most revered religious leaders and greatest political and social figures have been tested, yet they persevered in their calling despite trials and tribulations.

We admire George Washington for the way he exuded love and compassion toward his troops during their long winter at Valley Forge. Martin Luther King Jr. is beloved for the fearless way he pursued his dream despite numerous threats on his life. Similarly, we must overcome all the challenges that arise in following our calling.

How to Make a Connection with Your Divinity

There are many methods for improving your spiritual receptivity. It is simply a question of discovering the approach that works best for you. Let's begin with one of the easiest techniques, which is simply to relax. This relaxation exercise will help you become more receptive, thereby improving your soul connection within.

Relaxation and repetition

The next few paragraphs are a summary of the relaxation exercise. The full text can be found in the Appendix A. The first few times that you perform this 10-minute exercise, you may want to ask another person to read it aloud for you, at a slow and deliberate pace. As an alternative, you can purchase a recording of the exercise from the authors' website.

With your seed thought in mind, lie on your back on the floor or on a firm bed. Focus your awareness on your toes and feet. Increase your concentration and become aware of any tightness or tension in your toes and feet. Now, consciously and completely relax the muscles in your toes and feet. Feel them becoming more and more relaxed, the muscles becoming softer and softer, letting go entirely, relaxing completely.

Repeat these steps of awareness and relaxation as you move up towards your head, individually relaxing your body parts. Relax your ankles, calves, thighs, pelvis, lower abdomen, upper abdomen and stomach, forearms, wrists and hands, upper arms, chest, neck, and head.

You are now fully and completely relaxed. Your body is weightless. The only sensations you feel are the subtle flow of the life energy and blood circulating through your body. Take a deep breath, inhale slowly and completely, and then fully exhale. Take several more deep breaths, inhaling slowly and completely, and then exhaling slowly and fully.

Place your total attention on your seed thought and concentrate until it becomes the only thought in your mind. Visualize that your heart has a mouth. Repeat your seed thought over and over, speaking it through both your heart's mouth and your physical mouth. Begin speaking your seed thought in a normal voice, and then repeat it more and more softly until you are only repeating it mentally. Continue with this mental repetition until you feel you are totally one with your seed thought. Feel your seed thought vibrating through every cell in your body, becoming one with your body.

Repeat this exercise whenever you feel inspired to do so. If you want the assistance of your subconscious, as well as your conscious mind, the best time of day to perform this exercise is right after you wake up in the morning and/or right before you go to sleep at night.

Pay attention to how you feel after completing this exercise. Does repeating your seed thought consistently produce positive effects, such as increased energy, vitality, joy, love, confidence, positive dreams and visions? Does this repetition make you feel uncertain, unclear, weighed down and conjure up unpleasant dreams or scenarios? Is the result somewhere in between?

Write down what you experience physically, the thoughts and imagery that come into your mind and the emotions that play upon your heart. As you practice relaxing, visualizing and verbalizing, over time, you will become more aware of and receptive to the spiritual messages coming through you. This process will also evoke a clearer sense of whether your seed thought is your calling.

Prayer

The most widely practiced method for finding a calling is prayer. Prayer is about creating and maintaining a personal relationship with the Divine. It is easy for you to talk with your friends and receive their advice and counsel. In the same way, create an intimate relationship with God. Any method of conceptualizing the Divine that makes Him or Her a palpable living presence in your life will help you to achieve this intimacy. If you think of God as your friend, beloved, Mother, or Father, the divinity within will respond to you in that way.

You may want to use one of the following to invoke His or Her response with regard to your calling.

Father, make my work a calling to serve You.

Divine Mother, fill me with your love
that I may serve you by serving others.

My Beloved, I want to serve in the way You intended.

Heavenly Father, I will reason, will and act, and guide my reason,
will, and activity to the right thing that I should do.

My Divine Friend, I work for you. I use the talents
You gave me to create heaven on Earth.

Prayer is about your personal relationship with God. Since everyone is unique, there are as many ways to pray as there are people in the world. Please bear in mind that prayer is simply the first part of your divine communion. After you pray, be quiet so you can begin to feel the divine response in your heart. When your quiet time after prayer is filled with inner peace, understanding, or joy, you will know that you have been heard.

At times it may seem your prayers have gone unheeded. On such occasions it is helpful to remember past experiences where a seeming lack of response was the perfect response and a blessing in disguise. You can acknowledge that God knows what is best for you by repeating the prayer of *Sri Gyanamata,* "Change no circumstance in my life; change me."

Charles has a friend named Carl who lost his job. Carl's wife, Frances, continued to work but they could not survive on her salary alone; they needed to use Carl's retirement money to supplement Frances' income. Carl was doing everything he could to find a job, including searching the employment ads, using an executive placement service, enduring many job interviews and praying diligently every day.

After a year had passed, Carl felt he was ready for a new job. During the course of the next interview, Carl knew he had found his new job. It was the perfect position, utilizing all his skills and knowledge. Many of the positions Carl had applied for during the previous year were for a salary considerably lower than what he had been making. This job offered the same salary as his most recent job. This scenario has occurred on two different occasions in Carl's life.

Another reason prayers may elicit no response is due to a conscious, subconscious or unconscious belief of unworthiness. People pray sincerely and deeply—asking for that which they desire—but then place a glass ceiling over their heads with feelings of unworthiness. In effect, they are saying, "God, I really want this, but I know I don't deserve it." They ask for 100 percent of God's blessings, but feel they really only deserve 10 percent of those blessings. Not surprisingly, they receive exactly what they believe they deserve—nothing more and nothing less.

If you want to increase your havingness, lovingly embrace whatever feelings you have regarding worthiness or unworthiness.

If you are not in a loving place, simply observe the place that you are in. Be quiet and sit with any unworthy feelings you are experiencing. Return to this quiet witnessing place whenever the feelings of unworthiness surface. There is nothing to do here. Man is made in the image of God and simply being with the feelings creates the miracle.

Visualization

One of our favorite methods to create a spiritual connection is through visualization. A great deal of scientific research has been done on visualization. Brain scans have confirmed that the neurological activity during an intense visualization is exactly the same as it is while physically performing that activity. In other words, the brain cannot tell the difference between vividly visualizing an action in your inner world and performing that action in your outer world. Many world-class athletes now repeatedly rehearse their performance through visualization before the actual event and have found that this visualization greatly improves their performance. Whatever you visualize yourself attaining will come to pass.

Begin the visualization process by lying down, which helps you become completely relaxed. Repeat the relaxation portion of the exercise we talked about earlier. You may want to ask someone to talk you through this exercise the first few times you do it or you can purchase a recording of the exercise from the authors' website.

Once you have relaxed completely, visualize yourself performing the activities required to manifest your seed thought. If you want to make your current work into your calling, then visualize yourself in the office or on the construction site, or wherever you work. If you have a new vocation in mind, visualize yourself engaged in that new endeavor.

Make the visualization as vivid and detailed as possible. Visualize everything going great—you are happy, smiling, energetic and fulfilled. Every task is accomplished easily and perfectly.

Keeping this happy, successful work picture in your minds eye, surround it mentally with the brightest, most comfortable white light you can imagine. Everything you are doing is now radiant with that light. Continue this visualization until your heart fills up with positive feelings. Feel this joy increasing and expanding from your heart out into the rest of your body and mind.

Repeat this exercise whenever you are inspired to do so. If you want to harness the power of your subconscious, the best time to do this activity is right before you fall asleep at night and/or right after you wake up in the morning. At these times your subconscious resources are the most accessible to your conscious mind.

After you have finished your visualization, write down what you feel physically—the thoughts and imagery that come into your mind, and the emotions that play upon your heart. Over time, your visualizations will become more powerful. You will develop a heightened awareness and receptivity to the spiritual messages coming through you and gain a clearer sense of whether your seed thought is your calling.

Affirmations

Affirmations are short phrases or sentences that you say over and over again with great conviction and faith—at first aloud, and then more and more softly—until you are repeating them mentally to yourself.

A powerful affirmation was spoken by Sir Winston Churchill during a particularly dark time during World War II. The Germans were regularly bombing England. Sir Winston had little in the way of material resources and weapons, yet he possessed the power of words uttered with strong conviction. He declared, "[N]ever give in, never give in, never, never, never, never—in nothing, great or small, large or petty—never give in except to convictions of honour and good sense. Never yield to force; never yield to the apparently overwhelming might of the enemy."[12] These words inspired the British to endure and eventually triumph against a much stronger military foe.

Your words, too, have great strength. Words are the foundation of your communication with others and your own thinking processes. Words are the filter that shapes your consciousness, perceptions, and reality. Your words and thoughts are the very fabric of your reality. The efficacy of affirmations is proof that man is made in God's image. As God's word created the world, so your words create your reality. Below are a few affirmations that may help you create a more rewarding tomorrow:

I am made in God's image and I claim my divine birthright.

*By sharing my prosperity with others, I open a
channel for perfect prosperity to flow through me.*

Divine Mother has a mission for me. I am Her willing instrument.

My Divine Friend loves me and takes care of me. I am His Servant.

I will serve the Lord in all my days, in every way.

My Divine Beloved is flowing through me, flowing through me.

Practice gratitude

Each night before you go to sleep and/or each morning when you first wake up—before you get out of bed—focus on what you are grateful for. Think thoughts that fill you with gratitude. Think of all the blessings in your life, of the people and circumstances for which you are grateful.

Look at your surroundings. If you are in a relationship, look over at your partner lying in the bed beside you. Be grateful for your relationship, for the love and support you give to—and receive from—your partner. If you have children, think about the joy they bring you. Think about your friends and what they mean to you. Be grateful for the material circumstances of your life. Be thankful for all that you have.

To deepen the experience, you might want to create a gratitude journal. Each night before you go to sleep, write down a list of the things for which you are grateful. You might want to include a short description of the benefits you feel flowing into you from each person, event or experience on your gratitude list. In the morning, reflect upon what you had written the night before.

Performing this ritual just before you go to sleep and/or right after you wake up harnesses the power of your subconscious mind to assist you in practicing gratitude. The more you are grateful, the more you open up the channels for abundance to flow to you.

Brahms' Method for Connecting with God

A fascinating conversation with the great composer Johannes Brahms is memorialized in a book by Arthur M. Abell entitled *Talks with Great Composers: Candid Conversations with Brahms, Puccini, Strauss and Others.*[13]

In that conversation, Brahms asserted that God cannot be contacted using willpower working through the conscious mind. God can only be contacted through the soul powers within. According to Brahms, Jesus was the son of God and "we are all sons of God, for we could not have come from any other source. The vast difference, however, between Him and us ordinary mortals is that he had appropriated more of divinity than the rest of us have."[14]

The power from which all great artists, all great world leaders and all great business leaders draw their inspiration is the same power that enabled Jesus to work his miracles. It is the power that created everything in the universe, including you and me; and Jesus taught us that we can appropriate it for our own use right here and now.[15]

This is what Jesus meant when he said, "Ask and it shall be given you, seek and ye shall find; knock and it shall be opened unto you." (Matthew 7:7)

Brahms' process of connecting with God—of appropriating the power of God—began with the realization that such power exists. "You cannot appropriate unless you believe that it is a real living Power and the source of our being." You can only know this through the soul power within you.[16]

Brahms continued by contemplating the fact that we are one with the Creator. Then he appealed directly to God and asked Him the three most important questions pertaining to our life here in this world: Where did I come from? Who am I, and where am I going?[17]

Brahms put himself in a semi-trance condition to get results— "a condition when the conscious mind is in temporary abeyance and the subconscious is in control, for it is through the subconscious mind, which is a part of Omnipotence, that the inspiration comes. I have to be careful, however, not to lose consciousness, otherwise the ideas fade away."[18]

In this dreamlike state or trancelike condition Brahms was hovering between sleep and wakefulness—still conscious but right on the border of losing consciousness. And it is at such moments that inspired ideas came to him.[19]

Brahms always "had a very definite purpose in view before invoking the Muse and entering into such a mood...Then the ideas which I was consciously seeking flowed in upon me with such force and speed, that I could only grasp and hold a few of them; I never was able to jot them all down; they came in instantaneous flashes and quickly faded away again, unless I fixed them on paper...I felt that I was, for the moment, in tune with the Infinite, and there is no thrill like it."[20]

This Omnipotent Power is in all of us and anyone who is capable of entering into that dreamlike state can connect with divinity, can appropriate the power of Spirit and bring it into their business.

How Do I Recognize My Calling?

How do you know your seed thought is your calling from God? One of the keys is to see how you feel after immersing yourself in your seed thought. In the end it is truly a matter of connecting with your heart.

What if you do not get a clear feeling one way or the other from these exercises? Then we suggest that you develop your ability to be fully present in each moment by paying closer attention to what is happening in your life. Awareness is a powerful tool for transformation.

Everyone has a part to play. Jesus said that not even a sparrow could fall to the ground unless it was a part of God's plan. (Matthew 10:29)

Each of us has had the experience of turning on the TV or the radio and hearing an answer to a question in our mind. A friend had just attended a week-long religious convention but the joy of the week was diminished by some unhappy experiences when she returned home. She was silently complaining when she turned on the radio and instantly knew that someone was listening. The song she heard was, "I Never Promised You a Rose Garden." Ask for God's guidance and pay attention to what happens in the world in response.

Having a calling is similar to being in love. When people are in love, they never feel tired. In fact, they may lie awake at night contemplating the next time they will see their beloved. When you connect to your business on a soul level, you open yourself to the tremendous well of divine energy within you.

Remember Scott Walker? He tapped into that deep well of seemingly endless energy that comes when you find your calling. During the period when Scott was developing NET, he was also seeing patients. Five days a week, Scott treated patients in his chiropractic practice. Early every morning, late every evening, and all day every Saturday and Sunday, he spent developing the seminars he would teach and the materials he would use to teach them. Yet, Scott was never fatigued.

Ali Kiran tells a similar story. Ali owns Kiran Consulting Group, a company that develops forecasting software to streamline business operations. The software optimizes supply and demand by determining how many people should staff a business at any particular point in time. For example, several major banks use Kiran software to determine how many tellers should be on duty at various times throughout the day. In addition to maximizing the efficiency of the business, Kiran software also improves the quality of life for both the employees and the customers they serve. Kiran's customers include Universal, Dell, Disney, Wells Fargo, and Bank of America.

On September 14, 2001, Ali founded a company named Exametric to develop forecasting software. During the five years he grew the company, Ali always felt an abundance of energy, but at the same time he was very calm inside. Ali said, "You feel in charge, that you can do things, you are in control of events, things happen at your command." This state of mind is reminiscent of the final lines in the poem "Invictus" by William Ernest Henley: "I am the master of my fate: I am the captain of my soul." In the fall of 2006, Ali sold Exametric to a larger company for a substantial sum of money.

Accepting Your Calling

In the end, you must decide whether to accept your calling. Once you accept your calling, it is time to manifest your vision—to make your seed thought a reality in the world. We call this *grounding your calling in the world.*

STEP THREE—
GROUND YOUR
CALLING IN
THE WORLD

CHAPTER 4

Your calling has provided you with a destination. Now you need to determine how to get there. This is where planning comes in. Without a plan, it is unlikely that you will reach your goal. Without a plan, it is unlikely that your calling will become anything more than a dream.

The Secret to Success

What does it take to become *really* successful? Malcolm Gladwell addressed this question in his book *Outliers: The Story of Success*. He investigated some of the most successful people of the past fifty years, and came to several startling conclusions. One of those conclusions is that innate talent is not as important as preparation. It all boils down to who is willing to work the hardest. "(T)en thousand hours of practice is required to achieve the level of mastery associated with being a world-class expert - in anything...

It seems to take the brain this long to assimilate all that it needs to know to achieve true mastery."[21]

Malcolm Gladwell then applies this ten thousand hour rule to two of the icons of success in our age: The Beatles and Bill Gates. In 1960, when The Beatles were a struggling high school rock band, they booked a gig in Hamburg, Germany. They had to play eight hours a night, seven nights a week. The fledgling band "performed for 270 nights in just over a year and a half. By the time they had their first burst of success in 1964... (the Beatles) had performed live an estimated twelve hundred times" — more than most bands do in their entire career.[22]

Bill Gates is another product of extraordinary opportunity. He began "to do real-time programming as an eighth grader in 1968".[23] By the time Bill Gates created his own software company, he had "been programming practically nonstop for seven consecutive years".[24]

Were The Beatles and Bill Gates talented? Undoubtedly. But what set them apart from their talented contemporaries were the opportunities they were given and their willingness to spend many hours perfecting their craft. As Gladwell concludes, working hard is what successful people do—success follows a predictable course.

You may be saying, "Hey, I don't want to be a superstar, I just want to make a bunch of money." We humbly suggest that these same principles hold true not only for those who are wildly successful, but also for everyone else who is successful.

Lee Milteer is a performance and productivity coach, author, and professional speaker. She has counseled and trained over a million people through her presentations. Walt Disney, AT&T, XEROX, IBM, Ford Motor Co., NASA, Federal Express, 3M, hundreds of government agencies, as well as scores of conventions and associations have retained her services to inspire and motivate their audiences with up-to-date wisdom.

While Lee is neither Bill Gates nor The Beatles, she has certainly done very well. How did she get there? Lee was very successful as a salesperson and people kept telling her "You should do sales training." For five years, Lee unwittingly prepared for this career change. She spent many hours in the library, reading about human potential, how to be successful, and how to improve your self image and self-esteem. Like many of us, Lee came from a dysfunctional family and she read incessantly to heal her own wounds. Over time, this self-interest expanded into a desire to help others.

Lee understood that as a sales trainer she would have to do public speaking and she was tireless in researching how to become a professional speaker. She obtained every professional speaker's materials that she could lay her hands on. Lee studied their body language and how they operated. She felt great clarity, focus, and energy because she knew this was the path she was going to take.

Lee sent letters out to anybody and everybody who hired speakers in her hometown. She offered to speak for free, and in a three-year period she spoke 157 times so she could learn how to do it well. She joined the National Speakers Association, and flew to Phoenix, Arizona, to attend one of their meetings. At the event, she connected with the members and asked questions to learn as much as she could.

While Lee did not have a business plan, she intuitively knew what she needed to do. If she wanted to be hired as a speaker, she needed to contact the companies that hired speakers. Lee sent them information and followed up. She contacted newspapers and constantly sent out brochures, and talked to people on the phone. Lee did everything herself because she was a one-person business.

She spoke anywhere about anything and everything to maximize her exposure.

Lee marketed herself locally for several years and spoke before lots of small businesses and real estate companies in her area. It was a lot of hard work. But she was willing to go through that much hard work and that is why she became successful.

Lee's big national break came with Career Tracks. The company gave her six months to prepare a presentation on the topic of image and self-projection. It was trial by fire. At the end of the one-day presentation Career Tracks decided whether or not to hire the speaker for more than that one day. At the end of her day, Lee's rating was higher than any of their speakers had ever received. This was particularly noteworthy considering Career Tracks had a stable of one hundred speakers.

Lee was given a one hundred-city contract to present the same topic, and she became Career Tracks' top-rated speaker. She worked as a subcontractor for Career Tracks for six years. Lee expanded her offerings, presenting all sorts of topics, including sales, coping with change, and dealing with difficult people. On an average day, she was in front of three hundred to nine hundred people. She was on stage from 9 a.m. to 4 p.m. Each day she spoke for five hours and forty-five minutes. She made presentations in different cities three or four days in a row, and she was on the road three weeks a month.

Lee put in the time and was given the opportunity to become the master of her craft. That is why she has been so successful.

When Kim Gay started her company, she was still employed full time and could only work on her business when she had a day off. As a consequence, Kim worked seven days per week from sunup to sundown—part of the time for her job, and the rest on her own business. When her business opened its doors, Kim worked six days per week—she did everything but deliver the products. Working hard is what successful people do.

The Magic of Business Plans

In 1955, Robert Merritt began working at the Renfro Hosiery Mills Company, headquartered in Mt. Airy, North Carolina. The company—now known as Renfro Corporation—manufactures and distributes socks for men, women, boys, girls, toddlers, and infants. The company sells socks through mass market, department store, specialty outlets and e-commerce channels. In 1965, Robert became president of Renfro and he retired in 1992. By that time about one in five Americans were wearing socks made by Renfro. The company had annual revenues of $276 million in 2006, the year it was sold to an outside investor.

In 1961, Robert took a course at Chapel Hill in strategic planning and created a long-range plan for Renfro as a homework assignment. At that point, sales were $5 million per year. He forecast a 15 percent annual increase in sales, which meant that sales would double in five years.

People in the company thought Robert was out of his head. They asked, "How do you know what will happen next year?" Robert was undeterred and told his staff that the company would need a budget for next year, so they created one. They prepared a budget for one year, a more generalized five-year plan, and a very generalized blue-sky 25-year plan. Robert now had a goal in the background and that goal was on paper. He made and distributed copies of it and he and his people measured themselves against it.

The magic was that it happened. Although Robert did not quite hit his goal of 15 percent per year every year, the growth rate averaged 13.8 percent per year over those thirty years. Just saying,

"This is how we want to grow, we have these objectives," will help you get there. It is all fiction, all made up, but it becomes your reality. Robert does not think it would have happened if his goals had not been written down.

Richard had a very similar experience with his business plan. According to Richard, "In 1984 I was interested in starting a mortgage company. I attended a Small Business Administration seminar for new businesses, and one of the presenters said that every business must have a business plan. This was before the days of fancy computer programs where you could just answer questions and fill in the blanks; but the Small Business Administration instructor was nice enough to provide me the formatting for the business plan he recommended.

"It required that I make assumptions about supplies, employees, rent, telephone, postage, and all the other expenses needed to run this kind of business. I also had to project revenue for the next five years. Since I had no experience making money in this business, it was an exercise in finding out what things cost and visualizing success. I took it seriously, but at the same time I did not know if it had any validity at all."

Richard continued, "Soon after I created the plan and borrowed $10,000 from my loving mother, I put the plan in a folder and forgot about it. Recently I was going through some old storage boxes and found it. It was yellowing around the edges, but still quite legible. I was awestruck by the information in the plan. Not everything had played out as I had foreseen. There was no mention, for example, of the small steps I took in growing the business. Nor did it mention the heartache I felt each time I seemed to take a step backwards. Yet, there it was in black and white. The numbers I had predicted were almost identical to what had transpired in that business for the first five years.

"Years later I attempted to greatly expand my mortgage business and learned another valuable lesson about business plans. I had already gone through the first stage of business development, was established and looked forward to the next step. I grew my company from six to thirty-five people and the business expansion was a disaster. There are many reasons why my growth process did not work out, but the biggest one is that I *had no plan!*

"In the years since, I have read that those who write business plans are about four times more likely to succeed than those who pass them by. Of course, I also believe that writing things down brings ideas into the realm of material creation and that is a very important first step in making things happen."

Ali Kiran felt it was imperative that he have a business plan to follow in developing his new company. He wanted to create the plan in a cost-effective manner, but he had neither the time nor expertise to construct his own plan. In a stroke of genius, Ali hired four graduate students who had won a business plan competition at San Diego State University. He paid the students $4,000 to prepare a plan for him. Ali reviewed the plan as part of his preparation before meeting with potential investors, but never provided them with a copy of it.

Ali also used the business plan as a high-level conceptual strategy rather than as a formal planning document. The most important part of the plan was the overall summary—benchmarks for the growth of the business. For example, how many bank branches they should obtain as clients each year. The business performed as well or better than the benchmarks for the first two years; and Ernst & Young named Ali Kiran the 2004 San Diego Entrepreneur of the Year.

Zachary Taylor received training at Robert Schwartz's school for entrepreneurs in Terrytown, New York. Robert Schwartz had conducted think tanks for IBM, American Airlines, and other major corporations. Zachary learned how to flesh out ideas and refine his financial projections in the process of creating a professional business plan and private-placement memorandum.

For each of his projects, Zachary creates a separate business plan. He uses the business plan format to help him assess where he is at and how things are going in the project, and to visualize his business goals and analyze whether he is on track with those goals. If Zachary is off track, he makes course corrections. Some people think of a business plan as a fixed map to live by. It is not set in concrete. You can adjust it, making it a dynamic document open to modification.

Perfect Your Knowledge

Be a willing student of your chosen vocation. Learn all you can— both on your own and through others.

Creating her own business was a new experience for Kim Gay. When she didn't know how to do something and didn't know someone who could help her, she sought a book on the subject. Since she knew nothing about business plans, Kim read a book on developing a business plan and then created one. She sought out the guidance of others on how to customize her business plan.

Kim put her assumptions into the business plan, monitored cash flow, and determined when she needed to buy a product, or hold off. She used others—for their financial skills more than anything else—including a person with an MBA in finance. After she started her business Kim took a class at Georgia State University on financials for the nonfinancial person.

Kim recommends engaging the services of a good banker, accountant and attorney when starting your business. Her accountant and attorney were women who owned their own businesses and they provided her with a great deal of valuable advice.

Robert Merritt attended management training programs to learn about accounting and setting objectives. The first program was for executive management conducted at the Wake Forest University (Winston-Salem, North Carolina) business school. He also completed the Executive Program at the University of North Carolina. The knowledge he gained through those programs proved invaluable when Robert became president of Renfro in 1965. Still later, in 1981, he attended the Advanced Management Program for three months, at the Harvard Business School. This rigorous training utilized Harvard's case study method.

Robert also sought the advice of the heads of other companies in town. It was a simple matter to determine who to ask for advice. He selected widely admired companies where people loved to work. Robert had discussions with their executives about how they ran their companies, and used this information in formulating what he wanted Renfro to be.

Each of these businesses was led by individuals with very different management styles and personalities, yet all were relatively successful. Robert asked the executives about specific issues, such as water rates, finding new employees and pay rates for knitting machine mechanics and secretaries. He absorbed a lot of information and then reflected on it. This was how he learned.

When Carl Terzian began his own PR business, eight local businessmen put up $50,000 to help get his business going, and they became his board of directors and business advisors. This group provided valuable advice regarding business judgment— Carl bounced ideas off of them and they opened doors for him. Five years later, the head of the group told Carl, "You don't need our advice anymore. Let's go get a loan so you can pay back our original investment, without interest, and the business will be totally yours." Carl also relies upon his minister for advice. He telephones his minister several times a week and they meet in person several times a month. Carl gauges what people say about his firm and performs course corrections based upon that information.

As a child, Patty DeDominic dreamed of being a teacher and a mother. Her father was a businessperson and business conversations at the dinner table were a part of her life when Patty was growing up. Ultimately, Patty also became a businessperson because she discovered she was good at it.

In 1972, Patty went to work for Task Force, which through a series of mergers became Adecco, now one of the largest staffing companies in the world. It was a good place to begin a career because it was a large company that utilized well-designed and proven business methods and strategies. Patty learned a great deal about the staffing business by working for a company that was one of the industry leaders. She was trained in the recruitment process, developed the candidate base and helped build a very high-producing office.

Subsequently, Patty worked for a market leader in the cosmetics industry, and learned a lot from that job too. But in 1979, she felt called to start a staffing business. Shortly thereafter, Patty was invited to be a partner in an executive search firm. The owners of the company recognized her as a producer, and this partnership allowed Patty to incubate her business ideas. It was like swimming with a life jacket on.

In 1981, Patty started her own staffing company, PDQ Careers. It seemed very natural for her to do this. She wrote her business plan on the back of an envelope and later transferred it to one sheet of paper. She knew that she wanted to be involved in day-to-day operations in addition to strategic planning. Patty remembers hearing Jimmy Carter say "Underpromise and overdeliver," and that is what she vowed to do. Using this quote as her template, Patty executed a "very unsophisticated business plan"—she did what she said she would do and then some. This worked well in the long run.

As her business grew, Patty realized that her knowledge needed to keep pace. She audited numerous classes at UCLA in business and entrepreneurship. Patty received advice from SCORE, the SBA's Service Corps of Retired Executives. She took finance for nonfinancial manager courses at USC. The practical steps that Patty used to reach her goal were developed through education and experience. Patty said "It is all about the golden rule and responsibility—looking out for others and taking care of yourself."

How did her continuous search for greater understanding impact Patty's company? There were more than fifty staffing companies competing for business in the Los Angeles market when she opened her business. Patty grew PDQ Careers into one of the largest private businesses in the U.S., with over 20 percent compounded annual growth year after year. When Patty sold the company, it had more than six hundred employees on payroll, and placed more than two thousand people in full-time jobs each year. PDQ Careers "owned" the Los Angeles staffing market. In 2006, Patty's business acumen was publicly acknowledged by the *Los Angeles Business Journal*, which named her CEO of the Year.

Vrajseh Lal belongs to a CEO group with fourteen other company executives. Since all are from different industries, they can talk openly about issues in their businesses, and help each other find solutions and strategies for success. Vrajesh has found this group extremely valuable in helping him address a variety of concerns in building his business. He has also hired consultants to create procedures and systems to optimize his business.

In 2001, Ali Kiran was a member of the Chairman's Roundtable, a nonprofit made up of CEOs of various companies who would meet to help each other solve problems. Within each group, no company could be in the same business as any other company in the group. That way, members were free to openly share the issues confronting their businesses, receive advice, and cooperatively develop a course of action to solve those problems.

At that time Ali was struggling with the decision of whether the software his company had developed should remain the property of Kiran Consulting Group or be marketed through a new company. Ali asked the Chairman's Roundtable what he should do. The other CEOs asked questions regarding his motivation and personal goals and the group helped him plan a strategy. They collectively determined that Ali should start a separate company to market the software.

Ali built a strong board of directors, which includes his two investors, an ex-Ph.D. student who is Ali's right-hand man, an adviser from the Chairman's Roundtable and Ali. The board meets each month, with informal breakfast meetings for two months in a row, followed by a formal board meeting the third month. All of the board members are comfortable with one another, which results in a free flow of information in a very harmonious atmosphere. They discuss the issues facing the company; everyone provides their perspective and advice and in the end Ali makes decisions based upon their input. There has never been any dissent among the board's members about the direction in which the company should go.

Ali is also an advocate of open communication in his personal life. He has always consulted with his wife before making business decisions and she has fully supported the decisions that were made.

As these stories demonstrate, there is great value in seeking out and engaging advisors who can provide impartial support and advice to your venture. Why reinvent the wheel? Most of what you will need to do has been done by someone else before. Your idea may be unique, but your accounting, legal, personnel and marketing issues are not. Ask others to assist you and, in time, you may be able to pay it forward.

Tools for Manifestation

Mark Myers is an accomplished goal setter. He sets very specific, written, attainable goals to bring each property to the next level, then achieves those goals in a step-by-step fashion. For example, Mark's initial goals for a property he does not yet have listed are: (1) find out everything you can about the potential client, including their motivation for selling and their ability to sell (i.e., do they have sufficient equity to conform to market pricing), (2) create first-rate marketing materials to present to the potential client, (3) obtain the listing on the property, (4) distribute the offering to the broadest qualified national pool of buyers and pit the buyers against each other to maximize the price and terms for the seller, and then (5) work doggedly to serve the buyer, seller and their respective advisors and ensure that the transaction closes. Mark said, "The secret to success is to take it step by step and to complete each step with the greatest professional skill. If you want to be paid as much as a prominent surgeon, then train yourself to perform like one."

Lee Milteer strongly believes that you create your reality with your thoughts. If she wants something, she gathers pictures of what she wants and puts them together on a vision board. She affirms that vision in her mind, regularly looks at the board and acts as if she has everything in those pictures now. In her mind, she affirms,

"That's mine, I claim it as mine, and it will manifest when the time is right." She knows that it is just a matter of time—she will own that, she will have that.

Everything in your life is a story you tell yourself. In the same way, everything about manifesting the elements of your life is a story you tell yourself. Lee tells herself, "I can have whatever I want." It all starts with belief. You have the power to be a manifester. Look at life as a big toy store. Lee is a phenomenal manifester. That is a conscious choice she made.

Every year Lee Milteer goes on a vision quest. She believes that success comes from asking intelligent questions. On her annual vision quest Lee asks herself, "What do I want to do this year— what do I want to manifest?" She travels to Sedona, Arizona, to be by herself. Lee stays in a rustic place, anywhere from two to five days, isolated, writing in a notebook, spending time in nature, and being silent. She also embarks on smaller vision quests regularly. Lee takes walks on the beach, where she says to herself, "This is what's going on—what do I want to do?"

Zachary Taylor creates daily, weekly, monthly, and annual lists of goals. All of the more immediate goals are related to greater goals. He reviews both the workload and timing of completion of that work for the people who are working with him. He prepares lists for them or has them prepare their own from his notes.

Zachary doesn't tell people how to do something unless it isn't done properly or in a timely manner. He simply monitors what needs to be done and makes adjustments where they are necessary, letting people exercise their own creativity.

Business is a vehicle and you should treat it like one. Check it on a regular basis to make certain everything is running right. Create a daily list of things to do in keeping with your timeline, goals and calendar. Check things off. What doesn't get done should be rolled over to the next day. This is a simple and fundamental way to make progress towards your goals.

Zachary measures his business efforts with the yardstick of his spiritual values. He tries to live by the Golden Rule. As long as you treat others the way you want to be treated yourself, things will be good. If you see God in others and communicate with that part of them, then life is beautiful.

Zachary believes in divine outcomes. When the path is not clear, walk in faith. When you walk in faith, then supernatural progress is achievable. You cannot always logically discern what the next step is. The toes know because they feel it out, the feet go with the toes and sometimes we have to follow our feet rather than our head. "Walking in faith" simply means to follow your intuition. This empowers you and strengthens your connection with the source of all that is.

Instinct and Intuition

Later in his career, Robert Merritt learned to trust his gut, and this often turned out to be the best judge of what was transpiring. He never made a decision he didn't have a gut feeling about. To us, trusting your instincts is the same as trusting your intuition. Is it possible for you to develop this ability? We believe you can. Like any muscle, the more you use your intuition, the stronger it becomes. In addition, there are certain practices that can dramatically increase your intuitive power. One of the best of these is meditation.

For Zachary Taylor, meditation is the antithesis of thinking— it is about *not* thinking. It is just sinking into a certain centeredness of your being beyond the realm of thought. It is a place where no thing exists. Scott Walker agrees. Meditation allows him to empty his mind so he can look at things through a more neutral set of eyes, rather than creating a paradigm and looking for things to support it. Understanding this helped Scott formulate new approaches to the mind/body phenomena.

Daily meditation allows Scott to connect with divine love. Love reveals things to him. When you love your patients, the right thing is often revealed. Meditation helps him enter into a state of love, which then engenders knowledge, and ultimately helps him make better clinical and business decisions.

Vrajesh Lal meditates most mornings and evenings. Meditation has helped Vrajesh develop his intuition and improve his decision-making abilities. This daily practice brings the added benefit of filling him with inner peace. A palpable calm exudes from Vrajesh and envelops everyone within his presence. This serenity fosters harmonious, productive business relationships.

Ali Kiran is the first one in the office, arriving at 7:00 a.m. each day. On most mornings, Ali meditates for at least thirty minutes before he starts work. He originally meditated at his desk, but his office had a glass door. As a consequence, Ali began using his niece's office, which was more secluded. He also meditates in the evening before going to bed. Ali relies upon his meditation-enhanced intuition for guidance in deciding what to do and when to do it. He said, "On some level you have to go to your intuition or you will make the wrong decision or have the wrong timing. You just know because you know."

Lee Milteer goes within and meditates to quiet herself. Sometimes she goes in and becomes totally silent, and other times Lee meditates because she needs an answer. Lee also meditates while walking on the beach, hiking in the woods or being with her animals. Meditation happens simply through connecting with something that is outside of and beyond your conscious mind. On occasion, Lee goes into meditation to manifest.

For Lee, manifestation is a specific, well-developed process which involves visualizing what she wants. Lee has found that she cannot manifest until she clearly defines the picture of what she desires. This picture is merely a reference for her brain. Your reference doesn't have to be a picture. It could be a feeling or a conversation with yourself about what you want. Whatever type of reference you prefer, it is necessary to have a reference in order to manifest it in your life. You don't know that you can do something until you have a reference for it in your brain.

Additional Tools

Robert Merritt learned early on to pay close attention to what was happening around him and, during the course of his business career, he linked this conscious skill with the power of his subconscious mind. Your subconscious works twenty-four hours a day but you may rarely be aware of what this powerful computer is doing. If you can find a way to urge your subconscious to process the information taken in by your conscious mind, you will reap tremendous rewards.

Frequently at night Robert would think about some novel situation or problem he had encountered that day. Right before he went to bed, Robert meditated upon it and asked himself "What is going on here?" The next morning ideas would come into his conscious mind, often accompanied by a request for more data. Robert learned not to rush a decision based upon this first set of ideas. He would gather more data for the captive computer of the subconscious mind and repeat the process. If the situation or problem was new to him, one way in which he would gather additional data was by asking others how they had dealt with a similar circumstance.

At networking events, Carl Terzian listens to people and asks questions; this helps energize him. He tries to set a standard with his words and actions and continually polishes this standard so he will be a worthy role model. As a result, he lives the kind of life and has the type of reputation that others aspire to. Carl finds the good in everyone and highlights that. Work habits are important—returning calls, writing notes, referring business. Public relations is really human relations—how you treat people—and Carl treats people very well. That is why he is the master of public relations.

Ali Kiran is a member of a temple in San Diego. Whenever he enters the temple, he internally bows and says "I am here, what do you want me to do today?" On most Fridays, Ali also goes to the prayers at the Islamic Center of San Diego. He prays for the best results, not necessarily his own interest. Ali wants to have real success rather than being contracted into self-interest. In the office, this quote is on Ali's computer—"Real success is the expansion we are all trying to achieve." On several occasions he sent the quote as an e-mail to all of his employees. Ali is always working to be better, and he sees a little progress over the years.

Ali was trained as an engineer and he paraphrased the second law of thermodynamics—whatever energy you put out comes back to you sooner or later. For example, it is in your own best interest not to hurt others. He asks himself, "Is this a good thing to do for everyone involved?" If he can't say "yes," he won't do it.

Ali also believes in helping others. Ten percent of everything he makes goes to charity. He is now pursuing other creative ideas and, if all goes well, Ali can help even more people.

Do Your Homework

For a number of months, Richard mentored Margaret Bourdette in the mortgage business. When they began working together, Richard suggested that Margaret map out both her personal and business life. Richard later came to call this process your "Homework."

Margaret began her Homework assignment by envisioning life as a successful mortgage consultant. She used a day planner to record everything she needed to do to fulfill her business and personal responsibilities while living a life that fed her soul. Margaret mapped out the next three months—hour by hour and day by day.

How much time would she spend marketing? When would she meet with clients? How long would it take to buy supplies, do the books, and commute to the office? Then Margaret added her personal responsibilities and needs. Would she still take her two children to school and to their after-school activities? What about time for exercise, a spiritual support group, healthy meals?

After mapping all of these activities into her day planner, Margaret realized there was simply not enough time each day to accomplish everything that needed to be done. To create more time, Margaret developed an abundance team, which included her husband, a friend to help pick up her kids and an au pair. By following the plan laid out in her Homework, Margaret reached her goal in twelve months. We have included the business portion of the Homework done by Margaret Bourdette in Appendix B.

We encourage you to make a chart of what your life looks like on a 24/7 basis for the first three months of your business. How much time will it take to go to the bank, sort through your mail, answer telephone messages and e-mails, go to the grocery store, cook, pick up or do your laundry and perform all of the other seemingly endless tasks you'll need to complete each week? Is there someone else who can assist with some or all of the non-work-related tasks for you, if need be?

Set down the details of your day—from when you wake up until you go to bed at night. Include your meals, family time, visits with friends, exercise, prayer, and meditation. Then superimpose your newfound business responsibilities. What do you need to succeed in this business? Write down the times of the week when you are going to be servicing accounts, traveling, investigating products or whatever else is required of you in your business venture.

People do a similar exercise each day when they review their day planner and make entries for the upcoming days and weeks. You, however, are creating a day planner for a business that does not yet exist. One benefit of doing your Homework is it will force you to conduct the research on what will be required to make a success of your new business. Knowing what you need to do hour by hour will help you succeed.

By doing your homework, you will become aware of areas in which you may need to stretch, as you pursue your calling. If your new venture requires that you be a great salesperson, take note of it. Perhaps you will need to be an accountant or a motivator. Introspect regarding your new roles in life. Do you have the talents required to be successful in these new situations? Do you like doing this sort of thing? Be honest with yourself. If the required skills are new to you, you either need to learn those skills or hire someone else to do those tasks for you.

The following exercise may be helpful in your process of introspection. Thinking about your business, list your preferences in the following four categories on a piece of paper. When you have finished, ponder your results.

<u>What I like to do</u>
<u>What I don't like to do</u>
<u>What I am good at</u>
<u>What I don't do well</u>

Personally and professionally, we all have our comfort zones—those things we like to do and at which we excel. Yet, to be successful in your new business enterprise, you may need to go beyond those comfort zones.

When Richard's friend, Ed Mello, started his personnel business, he told Richard many stories of how he was networking with the people he already knew in the technology business. Richard said, "Ed had been there when the technology folks were in desperate need of programmers and team leaders, but the industry had gone south and there were no jobs. In spite of this, Ed worked and worked his leads.

"I asked Ed if he had considered moving his emphasis to another industry. I also asked if he had developed a personal relationship with any of the contacts he already knew. I knew the answer. Ed had relied on his phone skills because that was within his comfort zone. Ed was a bit introverted and had more than two decades of experience selling on the phone.

"He needed to cast his net deeper by developing personal relationships, and wider by going into fields that he did not already know. Ed and I stay in touch and he recently told me that he is having the most success he has ever had in the new field he is marketing to."

When you stretch—when you go beyond your comfort zones—you will find a whole new world of opportunity and abundance waiting for you.

Be of Service to Others

Whether you already have a business—or are thinking about going into business—it's helpful to ask yourself: "How can my business be more about serving others?" When you put others first, you cannot help but succeed. Many of our interviewees spoke of the importance of serving others.

Before Lee Milteer goes on stage, she envisions her audience and asks that her higher self connect with their higher selves. "Allow me to be of service, say and share the right things to empower these people to achieve, to learn, to know." Lee opens herself up to being a channel and something bigger than her takes over when she is on stage. It is not just what she says—there is a collective energy happening. Lee has the intention to be of service—to channel the light—and that is exactly what happens.

In his chiropractic and NET seminar businesses Scott Walker says that any decision he makes must also benefit the other person. He first looks at whether it will benefit others—if not, he drops it. If it works out for others, then Scott looks in depth to see if it will also benefit him. He sees a spark of God in the people he deals with, especially his patients. When Scott sees God in everyone, everything is put into a beneficial perspective.

Recently, Richard was called upon to make his business more of service to others. Says Richard, "One of my properties was experiencing a dramatic increase in tenants leaving for other properties. Not only was this causing a drain on our bottom line, but it also left me wondering if we were not properly serving the people who were leaving.

"I arrived at the property and had a meeting with the entire staff. I asked them what we were trying to achieve. 'Maximize profits.' they replied. I did not disagree with them. Every business needs to make money and everyone in business should have profit as a goal. Yet, nobody could tell me *how* we were going to increase profits. I told them we could only increase profits through increasing tenant satisfaction. Then the ideas started flowing.

"We decided to speak to all tenants before their leases expired about staying with us. It turned out that many of them had minor complaints. They did not see why we were increasing their rents when we did not fix up their apartments. We began to address their individual needs, whether it was for a new appliance or carpet cleaning. The results were fantastic. In just a few months we were back to a full occupancy with virtually no one wanting to leave."

Service to others is a form of enlightened self-interest. If you are always looking for how you can better serve others, you will always have plenty of people to serve. By helping others get what *they* want, you will get what *you* want.

As Mark Myers said, the secret to success is to take it step by step—this simple process has worked for his senior housing business—it can work for you. Let's review the steps for grounding your business vision in the world.

There is no substitute for hard work. Creating a business plan will help you chart your course. Learn all you can from others, and through books and classes. Utilize some of the many tools available for manifestation. Develop your intuition, which will be your guide when you need to make tough decisions. Do your homework so you know what will be required of you, what you're good at and what you should have others do for you. Be of service to others. If you do these things, you will succeed.

The good news, is when you are living your calling, your life is lived in a sacred space. You are energized and invigorated. It is a pleasure and a privilege to serve others. The long hours you work are a joy, not a burden.

Making a commitment to your business is a natural next step when you are living your calling, when you are celebrating your life. Tremendous power flows into and through you when you make that commitment.

STEP FOUR — MAKE THE COMMITMENT

CHAPTER 5

You have received your seed thought, made it your calling and undertaken the task of grounding your calling in the world. Now you are ready for the final step in the process of turning your business vision into a reality. This involves making a commitment to build your business into a wellspring of spiritual and material abundance. There are actually two parts to this commitment ceremony and we call them the contract and the covenant.

The Contract — Your Commitment to Yourself

So what is the big deal about commitment? Simply put, it is the key to personal success.

As we learned earlier with the 10,000-hour rule, hard work is a necessary element for success. Yet, nearly everyone who has ever been successful came to a point where they felt like they could not go on, that there was no point in continuing their business, in spite of the many hours they had devoted to it. Regardless, they did not break their commitment to themselves. What separates successful people from those who fail in business is that successful people simply refuse to give up.

Patty DeDominic said "Resiliency is an essential quality for survival in business these days, especially for U.S. businesses." You will get knocked down from time to time. The question is this: How quickly do you bounce back up? There has to be a practical, day-to-day balance of hard work coupled with spirituality. When the going gets tough, simply refuse to give up. That's what commitment is all about.

One day, Scott Walker and his wife looked at each other and knew they were going to mortgage their house and put all their money into his NET seminar business. They had discussed doing so on a number of occasions, but to actually do it involved a much deeper level of commitment. Scott was already committed internally—he knew in his heart that this was the path for him to follow. When they put their money "where their mouth was," Scott also became committed externally. It's like the old saw about breakfast—when you eat bacon and eggs, the chicken is involved but the pig is committed.

Kim Gay made a similar financial commitment and took comparable risks when she began her business. She withdrew all of her 401(k) retirement money and used those funds to buy the medical beds she would rent out to her customers. Once Kim made this commitment, the real work began. Kim worked seven days a week juggling her job and her fledgling company. She began working full time at her business in January and hired a delivery person in July. Shortly thereafter, Kim hired a nurse to support her sales efforts and the company began to grow by leaps and bounds.

Robert Merritt talked about commitment in terms of taking risks. It is very hard to take a risk that might result in losing money, yet doing something is more productive than doing nothing. What works is taking a chance. In business, the people who stick their necks out and *do* something are influential. You have to take risks.

In 1978 Robert did something that took him far out of his comfort zone. He attended a lecture given by Jim Farr, a Ph.D. psychologist. In that talk, Jim said "I could teach you how to operate in the world, manage time, manage a workforce, and set objectives, but if you are an S.O.B., then you would simply become a more skillful S.O.B. You need to work on your inner world that causes you to be an S.O.B., or whatever else you are that stands in the way of your success."

Robert took a leap of faith and signed up for the self-awareness workshop produced by Farr & Associates. At the workshop there were exercises that put each person in touch with their inner self.

This was the beginning of Robert's journey into self-exploration. He was so impressed with the experience that he sent his entire management team to the workshop, and they came back glowing. Then their wives went, followed by their secretaries. As a result, the management team at Renfro became honest and open with one another and was much more effective. They began sharing, criticizing and taking risks. Robert sent all of the supervisors at Renfro through the self-awareness training. The company was transformed. People from other companies in town came to work for Renfro because they heard people enjoyed working there.

This commitment involves far more than simple perseverance. By entering into a contract, you affirm your deep and abiding agreements to manifest your seed thought, your calling, and your plans for the unfolding of your business. There is a magic that happens as a result of making this commitment that goes way beyond anything your rational mind can understand.

> *Until one is committed, there is hesitancy, the chance to draw back, always ineffectiveness. Concerning all acts of initiative (and creation), there is one elementary truth, the ignorance of which kills countless ideas and splendid plans; that the moment one definitely commits oneself, then Providence moves too. All sorts of things occur to help one that would never otherwise have occurred. A whole stream of events issues from the decision, raising in one's favor all manner of unforeseen incidents, meetings and material assistance, which no man could have dreamt would have come his way... Whatever you can do, or dream you can, begin it. Boldness has genius, power and magic in it! Begin it now.*
>
> —W. H. Murray[25]

Vrajesh Lal said don't spend time thinking about "what if." Just do it. With any idea, you have to be committed from the beginning. Commitment itself is the driving force. If you feel good about the idea and it makes sense to you, go for it. The odds of success are lowest when you are starting out. Get committed to the idea, and before you know it, you will be successful.

Kim Gay formulated a business concept and began developing her plans to make that dream a reality. Then things magically fell into place. She realized it was necessary to procure a reasonably priced medical bed. The same day Kim had that thought she received a phone call from a manufacturer of medical beds in Florida that wanted to buy her employer's products as a supplement to their own product line. Kim asked about their product line and the responses convinced her that this was the product line for her own company. This happened over and over again. She would have an idea, start thinking about it and get a phone call that helped her implement the idea.

On the day she officially opened her business, Kim had a small booth displaying her products at a healthcare association convention. The Board Chair of the association came by and they started talking. It turned out he was the CEO of a small nursing home chain. He immediately gave Kim an appointment, which lead to business. It was a great way to start—with a small customer who would provide the experience she needed to work out the kinks in her business. Shortly thereafter, Kim received another, very large nursing home chain, as a client. As W. H. Murray said, all manner of people and events come to your aid once you have made the commitment.

The Importance of A Personalized Written Contract and Covenant

In chapter 4 we wrote about the magic of business plans. Robert Merritt, Ali Kirin and Richard all experienced similar results after creating a written business plan - their businesses performed as projected in their business plans. Writing down their goals helped make those goals concrete and achievable. In the same way, having a written contract and covenant will help you to concretize and achieve your business goals.

Throughout *The Prosperity Game* we have encouraged you to discover what is personally true for you and to live in that truth. This also applies to your contract and covenant. You are a unique individual and have a personal relationship with the divine. Your individuality should be reflected in the language you choose for your contract and covenant. These are living, breathing agreements that reflect who you are and how you relate to the divine. They are a celebration of you and your co-creation with divinity and a reflection of your unique contributions to life.

Below are Richard Fishman's contract and covenant for his real estate business, which have worked extremely well for him. However, your covenant and your contract should be written by you in your own words so that they truly reflect your commitment to yourself and your commitment to the divine.

Richard's Contract:

I, Richard A. Fishman, have received a Seed Thought from the Lord through my body, heart and soul. This Seed Thought is, you need to invest in real estate. This thought continues to grow in my heart and mind, filling me with inspiration and enthusiasm and giving me great joy each time I contemplate it. Through introspection and examination, the thought develops in my awakened mind into, create affordable, attractive housing in a way that is profitable. I will create a practical business plan for acquiring real estate and do my Homework on a personal level so I can uncover any potential obstacles to the creation of this business. I will work on my business so it becomes a fountain of spiritual and material abundance.

Richard Fishman   Date

Richard said, "My contract is a living document. Even though it governs my ambitions in real estate, I review it periodically to make certain I remain committed to its execution. Whenever I repeat the words of my contract, my commitment to the business is reinforced and reinvigorated. This contract, like many others, may have a beginning, middle and end. One day I might decide that this contract can be assigned to someone else. Perhaps my children will want to continue my business or I might sell the business to someone else. Alternatively, I might be called to another seed thought. For now, this is the endeavor to which I am personally, deeply committed."

By applying the scientific laws of success, you will obtain results—you will achieve financial abundance. Either consciously or unconsciously, all successful people go through the steps we have outlined. They find a seed thought, make it their calling, ground their vision in the world, and make a personal commitment to business success. However, by entering into a covenant with the Divine, you link your material life and your spiritual journey, ensuring greater riches in both realms.

The Covenant—Your Commitment to Spirit

To experience the highest levels of success and fulfillment, go beyond your personal commitment and make a covenant with Spirit. Vow that your business will play a central role in your divine mission on earth. When you make your business a divine business, you open to previously undreamed-of possibilities and rewards, far beyond anything that can be obtained through personal effort alone.

Richard's Covenant:

With open eyes and a willing heart, I now enter into a contract with God and my highest self to successfully complete this Divine Project—the creation of my real estate investment business.

_____   _____

Richard Fishman   Date

On a daily basis, Richard reviews his covenant and then affirms: "I will follow the road you have given me through the Seed Thought and Calling and will use my God-given talents to make it successful. I accept this journey as coming directly from You and will do my best to fulfill my duties to You. It is my privilege to express unqualified love and spiritual ambition. I will not be overly concerned with the results. If the results are not immediately forthcoming, I will be patient for however long it takes. When results do come, as I know they will, I will be ever thankful for Your blessings and accept them as coming from You."

Ed Mello tested the value of his covenant with God in the crucible of trying times. He had enjoyed modest success as a commissioned agent in a personnel company. Unfortunately, the tech bubble of the 1990s collapsed and Ed's company looked for ways to quickly reduce overhead. Without any advance warning, Ed was thrown overboard, jettisoned as dead weight.

Ed thought carefully about his situation and decided he wanted to go into business for himself. With financial backing from a friend, he dove into the entrepreneurial world by starting his own headhunting company with the gusto often seen in fledgling entrepreneurs.

Six months later, Ed was at the end of his rope. The bills were mounting and money was scarce. He couldn't sleep at night and he was questioning the wisdom of starting his own business. Again, this scenario is very common in new businesses.

To make matters worse, Ed's family had a new addition. In normal circumstances, this would be a source of great joy. To a beleaguered Ed, however, this new child was simply another mouth to feed and an added expense that he could ill afford at that particular time. He became increasingly distressed and anxious.

Ed discussed this predicament with his mentor, Richard. To Ed, it was simply a matter of "closing a few deals." In numerous conversations, Richard reminded Ed of his covenant with God. Ed had promised to provide exceptional service to his clients and leave the results to the Big Boss. Richard insisted that results would come if Ed simply played his part.

Each time Ed reflected on his agreement with God, he reinforced his commitment to the headhunting business. Peace filled him to overflowing when he remembered that God was his business partner and this was his divine calling. Even though he frequently felt like quitting, Ed persevered. He drew strength from God in meditation and prayer. He used that strength to stay true to his game plan in the rough-and-tumble world of day-to-day business.

By connecting with the Source of all that is, Ed stuck it out and created a flourishing business. He successfully combined his spiritual and material aspirations.

Reinforcing Your Covenant

The spiritual millionaires we interviewed for this book have found a variety of ways to maintain their covenant as a living, breathing, vital, and vibrant commitment.

Patty DeDominic prays for guidance and practices gratitude by giving thanks for what she has.

In addition to meditating on a daily basis, Vrajesh Lal reads spiritual books and practices being grateful to God. He does everything he can think of to connect directly with God. Whenever he remembers to do so, Vrajesh imagines he is with God, feeling His presence.

When he was younger, Vrajesh would only look for God when things were not going well. Now he feels God's presence and is in tune with God most of the time—in good and in bad times. When challenges come up, Vrajesh remembers that God always brings about what is right for him and this helps Vrajesh maintain a positive attitude.

Vrajesh feels very blessed by God. Business is always challenging but he sees these challenges as an opportunity for both material and spiritual growth. The challenges in business help Vrajesh be more in tune with God and he believes that through his ever deepening meditation and practicing the presence of God, spiritual and material success will become one and the same for him.

Scott Walker has a sign above his reception area that states, "God does the healing, the doctor takes the fee." This helps him remember that this is God's business, and he is just the office manager. Scott tries to make decisions based upon what is the right thing to do, even if doing so will cost him money.

Business is the daytime prayer, and meditation is the nighttime prayer. Doing business for the greater good of mankind is your daytime prayer. The goal Scott and his wife have for their chiropractic practice is to do everything they can to make their patients well, as fast as they can. They strive to be totally in service to their patients; to put their heart, mind and soul wholly into their patients, not themselves. The daytime prayer is all about helping others and supporting God's children. Scott concluded his interview with this quote from Swami Vivekananda, "He alone serves God who serves all others".

Reap the Richest Harvest

A number of years ago a man phoned Carl Terzian out of the clear blue on a Friday. His company manufactured a facial cream for women and was going to give Carl's PR company a $50,000-per-month retainer. The new client wanted Carl in Las Vegas the next night for a black-tie dinner for their monthly meeting with their top producers. After the call, Carl announced the good news to his staff.

At the festive dinner, the facial cream manufacturer's chairman said to Carl, "I have been told that you have very good political contacts with a certain senator." He then named the senator and asked "Do you know him?" Carl said "Yes." The chairman suggested, "I have a request—I need a federal pardon." Carl excused himself, located a phone, and called an associate to check on the background of the chairman. They discovered that a number of state attorney generals were pursuing the chairman for running Ponzi schemes.

The president of the company had given Carl the first month's check for $50,000 and a second month's advance, which Carl had planned to donate to his church on Easter Sunday. Carl tore up the checks, and terminated their relationship the next day. At that time the client would have been a huge asset for Carl's firm and the loss was a blow to the small company. However, other clients—whose behavior and ethics were more appropriate—soon appeared to take their place. Within a few months, the face cream manufacturing company was shut down.

Carl had a similar experience with a billionaire client. Unfortunately, this client was a rude person with a miserable personal life. Even though Carl had assigned eight staff members to this client's account, he decided the man's business and personal ethics were not in alignment with his own, so Carl terminated their relationship. When he announced the decision to his staff, Carl said no one would be laid off as a result of this client loss. Indeed, while Carl looked for new business, employees took cuts in their salaries to keep the staff who had served the client on board. Phone calls came in and doors started to open. It took only six months to replace this man's business.

In the early 1980s, when Patty DeDominic's company, PDQ Careers, had less than $10 million in annual revenue, she had a billionaire client who generated $1 million of business annually. This client had discriminatory policies and overtly sexually harassed female employees. At that time, corporations often tolerated such discrimination and harassment, but Patty felt the client's employment policies and behavior were wrong. She knew it was not in their best interest to retain that client.

PDQ held a company retreat and reviewed their mission statement, which was *staffing partners to America's finest employers*. With that in mind they did not rebid the billionaire client when it came time to do so. Other business came along which replaced the business of that client.

Some years later, PDQ Careers had a client who generated $4 million worth of business each year—a substantial portion of their annual income. The PDQ employee who serviced the account had a personal connection with the client. Unfortunately, the employee continually violated all of PDQ's values. Patty let the employee go at the risk of losing the client, because it was the right thing to do. She did not lose the client.

Have Faith in Your Mission

You are led down the path that is for your greatest good. Everything happens to fulfill your mission on Earth.

Richard has his own testimony with regard to this point. "Years ago, while attending college, I studied a field called regional science. My focus was to study the growth of urban areas and develop knowledge of how cities grow and decline. After working briefly in this field, I began a long career in the real estate finance business. While I often thought my regional science degree might have been a waste of time, I also felt there was a higher purpose— that God was directing me. I ventured into real estate investment and noticed that I had a fully developed understanding of how to evaluate the growth patterns in the cities where I was looking at potential properties and also knew how to finance the deals."

A Short Fable

Once upon a time there was a shepherd who roamed the hills grazing his sheep for months on end. This vocation afforded him plenty of free time, and he prayed to God for a purpose greater than keeping sheep. One day the shepherd was startled to hear a voice command, "Move that rock." Indeed, the man was praying next to a large boulder. When the shock wore off, the shepherd began to doubt that he had heard anything at all, much less a divine command. He thought, "This rock is so huge, God would certainly not ask me to move it."

The shepherd began again to pray for a purpose, even more fervently than before. And again he heard, "Move that rock." This time the Voice was more stern and commanding. He thought, maybe God is answering my prayer after all. So the man decided he would try to move the huge boulder. Whenever he was not busy tending to his flock, the shepherd would try to move the rock. As the days and hours passed, he pushed and pushed. Yet, the boulder never moved, not even an inch.

Finally the shepherd returned to his village with his sheep to prepare for winter. That night there was a terrible storm and lightning struck his home. The home began to collapse and everyone rushed for the threshold. The front door began to buckle and the shepherd held the door frame in place until all of his family had escaped to safety. His arms, strengthened by following the divine inner command to move the rock, enabled the shepherd to save his family.

Once you have made a covenant with the Divine, you have the best possible business partner. Whatever comes your way is for your highest good—there are no mistakes. Each day you grow in Spirit while you fulfill your God-given mission. You discover the true meaning of success.

Like the spiritual millionaires who you have come to know through these pages, you are truly blessed.

ABOUT THE AUTHORS

Richard Fishman

Richard Fishman received his B.A. and M.A. degrees from the University of Pennsylvania in 1979 and subsequently worked for the city of Philadelphia in its Community Development Program. In 1984 Richard began his career as a licensed California real estate broker by founding a real estate finance company in the San Francisco Bay Area. Richard began purchasing commercial real estate as an investment in 1989 and today he owns thousands of apartment units worth in excess of $300 million. These properties are located throughout the U.S.

Many years of meditation and prayer have shaped the spiritual philosophy which Richard applies to his business: "Maximize revenue through tenant satisfaction."

Richard believes he can profoundly influence people's lives by providing them with a great place to live. Through focusing on serving his tenants, Richard has grown his real estate investment business from a 6 unit apartment complex to over 3,300 apartment units.

Richard's company, the Valcapgroup, is headquartered in Houston. Valcapgroup's investment strategy is to purchase previously overleveraged apartment complexes and return them to a service oriented model - providing good housing for tenants and a return for investors. Richard believes that rental housing will continue to be a growth industry for the foreseeable future.

Over the years numerous individuals have sought Richard's aid and advice in their pursuit of material abundance. Through successfully coaching many entrepreneurs, Richard came to understand that there is a path which leads to success. That understanding became the seed thought for *The Prosperity Game*. Richard has presented the concepts contained in *The Prosperity Game* to a variety of audiences, including local church meetings and real estate seminars in the San Francisco Bay Area.

Charles Werner

Charles Werner has combined a 30 year career as a business attorney with regular practice of meditation and a lifelong interest in self-development. Through his legal practice in San Francisco, Honolulu and Los Angeles, Charles has helped numerous entrepreneurs manifest the abundance they envisioned in businesses ranging in size from startups to middle market companies. Charles relies on insight and intuition as valuable adjuncts to his analytical skills.

In Hawaii, Charles taught public speaking to undergraduates at Chaminade University, and business communication to undergraduates and business law to MBA program graduate students at Hawaii Pacific University. Charles has given presentations and conducted seminars in California, Hawaii and New Zealand on a variety of topics.

Charles served as an officer on the board of directors of two nonprofit organizations: the Berkeley Holistic Health Center and

Homeless Solutions. He is currently the Secretary of the board of directors of Step Up On Second, which provides housing and social services for the mentally ill homeless in the Los Angeles area.

Charles continues to practice law in California. He also provides consulting services to business leaders who want to enhance the performance of their businesses, improve their personal leadership skills and/or transform their company into a game changer in their industry. More information on his company, The Ultimate Business Advantage Leadership Consulting, can be obtained from its website, www.tubalc.com.

ACKNOWLEDGMENTS

Thank you Carl Terzian for your heartfelt foreword and abiding friendship.

We owe a special debt of gratitude to our interviewees, whose knowledge and insights have contributed so much to The Prosperity Game. Thank you Stephen Crisman, Patty DeDominic, Kim Gay, Edna Hennessee, Ali S. Kiran, Vrajesh Lal, Robert Merritt, Mark L. Myers, Lee Milteer, Drake Sadler, Zachary Taylor, Carl Terzian and Scott Walker for your time and expertise.

Thank you Peter Economy and LinDee Rochelle for your thoughtful editing, which improved this book.

The Prosperity Game owes its greatest debt to our wives. Thank you Susann for your loving patience and help. Thank you Peggy for your brilliant insights, which encourage me to go deeper.

APPENDIX A

Relaxation and Repetition Exercise

The first few times that you do this 10 minute exercise, you may want to have another person read it to you, at a slow and deliberate pace. As an alternative, you can purchase a recording of the exercise from the authors' website.

Lie on your back on the floor or on a firm bed. Focus your awareness on your toes and feet. Increase your concentration and become aware of any tightness or tension in your toes and feet. Now, consciously and completely relax the muscles in your toes and feet. Feel your toes and feet becoming more and more relaxed, the muscles becoming softer and softer, letting go completely, relaxing completely.

When your feet and toes are totally relaxed, move your awareness and concentration into your ankles, again becoming aware of any tightness or tension in your ankles. Consciously and completely relax the muscles in your ankles. Feel your ankles becoming more and more relaxed, the muscles becoming softer and softer, letting go completely, relaxing completely.

When your ankles are completely relaxed, move your awareness up into your calves, concentrating on any tightness or tension you feel in your calves. Consciously relax the muscles in your calves. Feel your calves becoming more and more relaxed, the muscles becoming softer and softer, letting go completely, relaxing completely.

When your calves are completely relaxed, move your awareness up into your thighs, concentrating on any tightness or tension you feel in your thighs. Consciously relax the muscles in your thighs. Feel your thighs becoming more and more relaxed, the muscles becoming softer and softer, letting go completely, relaxing completely.

When your thighs are completely relaxed, move your awareness into your pelvis, concentrating on any tightness or tension you feel in your pelvis. Consciously relax the muscles in your pelvis. Feel your pelvis becoming more and more relaxed, the muscles becoming softer and softer, letting go completely, relaxing completely.

When your pelvis is completely relaxed, move your awareness into your lower abdomen, concentrating on any tightness or tension you feel in your lower abdomen. Consciously relax the muscles in your lower abdomen. Feel your lower abdomen becoming more and more relaxed, the muscles becoming softer and softer, letting go completely, relaxing completely.

When your lower abdomen is completely relaxed, move your awareness into your upper abdomen and stomach, concentrating on any tightness or tension you feel in your upper abdomen and stomach. Consciously relax the muscles in your upper abdomen and stomach. Feel your upper abdomen and stomach becoming more and more relaxed, the muscles becoming softer and softer, letting go completely, relaxing completely.

When your upper abdomen and stomach are completely relaxed, move your awareness into your forearms, wrists and hands, concentrating on any tightness or tension you feel in your forearms, wrists and hands. Consciously relax the muscles in your forearms, wrists and hands. Feel your forearms, wrists and hands becoming more and more relaxed, the muscles becoming softer and softer, letting go completely, relaxing completely.

When your forearms, wrists and hands are completely relaxed, move your awareness into your upper arms, concentrating on any tightness or tension you feel in your upper arms. Consciously relax the muscles in your upper arms. Feel your upper arms becoming more and more relaxed, the muscles becoming softer and softer, letting go completely, relaxing completely.

When your upper arms are completely relaxed, move your awareness into your chest, concentrating on any tightness or tension you feel in your chest. Consciously relax the muscles in your chest. Feel your chest becoming more and more relaxed, the muscles becoming softer and softer, letting go completely, relaxing completely.

When your chest is completely relaxed, move your awareness into your neck, concentrating on any tightness or tension in your neck. Consciously relax the muscles in your neck. Feel your neck becoming more and more relaxed, the muscles becoming softer and softer, letting go completely, relaxing completely.

When your neck is completely relaxed, move your awareness into your head, letting go of all tension and emotions. Consciously and completely relax your mind, letting go of all thoughts. Feel your mind becoming more and more relaxed, emptier and emptier, letting go completely, relaxing completely.

You are now fully and completely relaxed. Your body is weightless. The only sensations you feel are the subtle flow of the life energy and blood circulating through your body. Take a deep breath, inhale slowly and completely and then exhale slowly and completely. Take several more deep breaths, inhaling slowly and completely and then exhaling slowly and completely.

Place your full attention on your seed thought and concentrate until it becomes the only thought in your mind. Visualize that your heart has a mouth. Repeat your seed thought over and over, speaking it through both your heart's mouth and your physical mouth. Begin speaking your seed see thought in a normal voice, and then repeat it more and more softly until you are only repeating it mentally. Continue with this mental repetition until you feel you are totally one with your seed thought. Then mentally ask *"Is this the right path for me to take?"* or declare *"Not my will, but Thy will be done"*.

Repeat this exercise twice each day for a week. If you want the assistance of your subconscious, as well as your conscious mind, the best time of day to do this is right after you wake up in the morning and/or right before you go to sleep at night.

Pay attention to how you feel after completing this exercise. Does repeating your seed thought consistently produce positive effects, such as increased energy, vitality, joy, love, confidence, positive dreams and visions? Does this repetition make you feel uncertain, unclear, weighed down, and conjure up unpleasant dreams or scenarios? Is the result somewhere in between?

Write down what you experience physically, the thoughts and imagery that come into your mind, and the emotions that play upon your heart. As you practice relaxing, visualizing and verbalizing over time, you will become more aware of and receptive to the spiritual messages coming through you and will gain a clearer sense of whether your seed thought is your calling.

APPENDIX B

Business Portion of Margaret Bourdette's Homework Plans for Growth

Definition of Success

- While it is true that "wealth isn't measured by money alone," financial freedom and prosperity are certainly a necessary component of success as I define it.
- Financial freedom and prosperity (one part of success) could be defined by "having enough money so one does not spend their vital life energy in constant worry or obsession about it." In other words ...
- To reach equilibrium where money is not the overriding concern.
- Further definition of success is a life in which "we make visible what without us, might perhaps never have been seen."
- Success includes the ability to discern one's Life Intentions and to take Authentic Action in achieving that higher purpose.

- Priorities and Goals, followed by Authentic Action, create a daily focus for us to reach success—One Step at a Time.

What would it be like to make $250,000 a year?

What would it look like on an hourly, daily, weekly basis?

How would I get from here to there?

How many loans will it take to make $250,000 a year?

$250,000 year @ $2,500 net per loan

= 100 loans per year

= 8 loans per month

= 2 loans per week

(Number varies based on net per loan.)

How would my life look?

My hours based on current schedule :

- MONDAY   9–2:30   5.5
- TUESDAY   9–4:00   7
- WEDNESDAY   9–2:30   5.5
- THURSDAY   9–4:00   7
- FRIDAY   9–4:00   7

TOTAL: 32 hours/week in daytime hours for first month (first 1–3 months).

Evening and weekend hours will be added.

- Time spent in setting up new office space will be taken from these hours.

Plan for Closing
2–3 Loans per Week

- 2–3 hours = Calls to qualified prospects
  - ◊ Realtors
  - ◊ Past clients
  - ◊ Friends/Family
  - ◊ Estimate 1 loan application scheduled per 2 hours of calls
  - ◊ Goal of 4 applications scheduled per week
  - ◊ Reduce prospect calls to minimum 1 hour per day on application days
- 1–2 hours = Work up loan for upcoming application
  - ◊ Run credit
  - ◊ Discuss products
  - ◊ Compare rates
  - ◊ Print disclosures, application, etc.
- 30 minutes = Study rate sheets, programs
- 30 minutes = Read and respond to email
- 30 minutes = Read and file mail
- 1 hour = Calls to processor, follow-up on files
- 1 hour = Calls to clients with pending loans
- 1 hour = Return calls, miscellaneous
- 8–10 hours minimum per day, to produce result of 2–3 loans per week
- First month 5 loans expected, balance of time spent setting up office space and systems
- Additional time evenings and weekends will be needed
- Driving time 30–60 minutes per day
- Application time taken from prospecting time; keep applications to 1–2 hours including driving

APPENDIX C

Contact Information for Interviewees

Patty DeDominic
805-453-7490
Website: www.dedominic.com

Kim Gay
Medinet Systems
2 Ravinia Drive
Suite 500
Atlanta, GA 30346
404-921-3732
Website: www.medinetsystems.com
Email: kim@medinetsystems.com

Ali S. Kiran
Website: www.kiran.com

Mr. Vrajesh Lal, CEO
Just for Wraps Inc.
5815 Smithway
Commerce, CA 90040
Telephone number 213-239-0503

Mark L. Myers
Senior Vice President Investments
Senior Director, National Senior Housing Group
Marcus & Millichap
8750 West Byrn Mawr Avenue, Suite 650
Chicago, IL 60631
773-867-1470
773-867-1510 fax
773-383-6821 mobile
mark.myers@marcusmillichap.com

Lee Milteer
Lee Milteer Inc.
2100 Thoroughgood Road
Virginia Beach, VA 23455
office phone: 757-363-5800
toll free: 800-618-6780
fax 757-363-5801
Website: www.milteer.com
Email: leemilteeroffice@gmail.com

Zachary Taylor
G-Force I.E.C.
Website: www.gforceiec.com
Email: ztaylor@gforceiec.com

Carl Terzian
Chairman of the Board
Carl Terzian Associates
Westwood Place
10866 Wilshire Boulevard, Suite 750
Los Angeles, CA 90024
310-207-3361
FAX 310-820-0626
Email: carl.terzian@carlterzianpr.com

Practitioners who have studied the Neuro Emotional Technique (NET) with Scott Walker
www.NETmindbody.com/for-patients/find-a-practitioner-near-you

The following people have requested that you respect their privacy and not attempt to contact them.
Stephen Crisman
Robert Merritt
Drake Sadler

In memoriam Edna Hennessee,
who left her body on March 22, 2011.

Endnotes

1   Rhonda Byrne, *The Secret*, (Atria Books, 2006).

2   Malcolm Gladwell, *Outliers: The Story of Success*, (Little, Brown and Company, 2008).

3   Alex Edmans, *The Link Between Job Satisfaction and Firm Value, With Implications For Corporate Social Responsibility*, forthcoming in the Academy of Management Perspectives, (August 17, 2012). Copyright © 2012 by Alex Edmans. By permission of Alex Edmans.

4   Towers Watson, *The Talent Management and Rewards Imperative for 2012, Leading Through Uncertain Times, The 2011/2012 Talent Management and Rewards Study, North America,* www.towerswatson.com. Copyright © 2012 by Towers Watson. By permission of Towers Watson.

5   Great Place to Work® Institute, *Transforming Into A Great Workplace, A Case Study Of Scripps Health*, (2011). Copyright

of Random House, Inc. Any third party use of this material, outside of this publication, is prohibited. Interested parties must apply directly to Random House, Inc. for permission.

11 http://en.wikipedia.org/wiki/Luxor_Las_Vegas.

12 http://en.wikisource.org/wiki/Never_Give_In,_Never,_ Never,_Never.

13 Arthur M. Abell, *Talks with Great Composers: Candid Conversations with Brahms, Puccini, Strauss and Others,* (Citadel Press Books, Carol Publishing Group, 1994). Copyright © 1955, 1987 by Philosophical Library, Inc. By permission of Philosophical Library, Inc.

14 Arthur M. Abell, *Talks with Great Composers: Candid Conversations with Brahms, Puccini, Strauss and Others,* (Citadel Press Books, Carol Publishing Group, 1994), 12–13. Copyright © 1955, 1987 by Philosophical Library, Inc. By permission of Philosophical Library, Inc.

15 Arthur M. Abell, *Talks with Great Composers: Candid Conversations with Brahms, Puccini, Strauss and Others,* (Citadel Press Books, Carol Publishing Group, 1994), 11. Copyright © 1955, 1987 by Philosophical Library, Inc. By permission of Philosophical Library, Inc.

16 Arthur M. Abell, *Talks with Great Composers: Candid Conversations with Brahms, Puccini, Strauss and Others,* (Citadel Press Books, Carol Publishing Group, 1994), 14. Copyright ©

1955, 1987 by Philosophical Library, Inc. By permission of Philosophical Library, Inc.

17 Arthur M. Abell, *Talks with Great Composers: Candid Conversations with Brahms, Puccini, Strauss and Others,* (Citadel Press Books, Carol Publishing Group, 1994), 5. Copyright © 1955, 1987 by Philosophical Library, Inc. By permission of Philosophical Library, Inc.

18 Arthur M. Abell, *Talks with Great Composers: Candid Conversations with Brahms, Puccini, Strauss and Others,* (Citadel Press Books, Carol Publishing Group, 1994), 6. Copyright © 1955, 1987 by Philosophical Library, Inc. By permission of Philosophical Library, Inc.

19 Arthur M. Abell, *Talks with Great Composers: Candid Conversations with Brahms, Puccini, Strauss and Others,* (Citadel Press Books, Carol Publishing Group, 1994), 9. Copyright © 1955, 1987 by Philosophical Library, Inc. By permission of Philosophical Library, Inc.

20 Arthur M. Abell, *Talks with Great Composers: Candid Conversations with Brahms, Puccini, Strauss and Others,* (Citadel Press Books, Carol Publishing Group, 1994), 69. Copyright © 1955, 1987 by Philosophical Library, Inc. By permission of Philosophical Library, Inc.

21 From OUTLIERS by Malcolm Gladwell. Copyright © 2008 by Malcolm Gladwell. By permission of Little, Brown and Company. All rights reserved. Page 40.

22 From OUTLIERS by Malcolm Gladwell. Copyright © 2008 by Malcolm Gladwell. By permission of Little, Brown and Company. All rights reserved. Page 50.

23 From OUTLIERS by Malcolm Gladwell. Copyright © 2008 by Malcolm Gladwell. By permission of Little, Brown and Company. All rights reserved. Page 51.

24 From OUTLIERS by Malcolm Gladwell. Copyright © 2008 by Malcolm Gladwell. By permission of Little, Brown and Company. All rights reserved. Page 55.

25 From *The Scottish Himalayan Expedition* by William Hutchison Murray. Copyright © 1951. (Orion Publishing Group). All attempts to trace the copyright holder of *The Scottish Himalayan Expedition* by William Hutchison Murray were unsuccessful.

Printed in the USA
CPSIA information can be obtained
at www.ICGtesting.com
JSHW082356140824
68134JS00020B/2104

9 781614 485803